Fun with Non-Fiction

Model Texts from Reception - Year 6

written by Betsy and David Maytham

CONTENTS

INSPIRING NON-FICTION WRITERS

DAVID MAYTHAM

Teaching non-fiction writing in primary schools has always been problematic. Yet writing for different audiences and purposes is not only a requirement of the British and a number of international curricula, it is also an essential skill in twenty-first century society. Employers need the next generation of their employees to respond quickly to briefs; to adapt their language to a range of contexts, audiences and purposes; and to deliver effective reports, presentations and buzzword-heavy product/service descriptions in an increasingly target-driven commercially-minded society. For me, effective non-fiction writing is an essential life skill. Schools have both a curriculum requirement and also a moral obligation to deliver this effectively.

To understand how to teach non-fiction writing effectively in primary schools, we first need to understand why children struggle with it. My belief is that there are four key underlying barriers children face with non-fiction writing:

Experience

First, and most crucial is **experience**. The average child experiences high quality non-fiction texts far less than they experience fiction. As a parent myself, I have hundreds of fiction books available at home and take great joy in reading my children a bedtime story each night. However, when I look across the bookshelf I'm often struck by the fact that the majority of these books are fiction. I'm sure I'm not alone!

As a primary teacher and now a consultant, I frequently challenge schools to consider these questions: if you were to track a child from Reception to Yr 6, which non-fiction texts would they experience during their school lives? Is there a good range of fiction and non-fiction? How often do we read or share non-fiction texts with our children, in comparison to how often we read narratives? In your classroom at the moment, how many fiction books are available and how many non-fiction? These are great questions to ask yourself and reflect on. When you do, I believe you will find that the majority of children have far more exposure to and experience of fiction than non-fiction in their daily lives.

It's not just the experience that matters; it's the **right kind of experience**. Take a text type like instruction writing. At a surface level, you might think that primary aged children should come into school with a rich experience of instructional writing. They may have read recipes, followed instructions on how to put together a toy and, hopefully(!), followed verbal instructions from adults in a range of situations. However, if you reflect on this a little more deeply, you will see that the experiences that children are receiving are very different to our expectations of the specific text type in the classroom. For example, a child who opens a toy at Christmas will nowadays most likely be faced with diagrammatic instructions, often with absolutely no words: a very different experience of instruction writing than the nicely formulated set of instructions we expect them to produce in class! In a multi-lingual world, this is a perfectly sensible way of overcoming the ever-increasing language barriers, but it doesn't help the children we teach learn to write a set of instructions. Children who don't read and explore a broad enough range of non-fiction texts are, as a result, often unable to use and apply the appropriate language features of non-fiction to their writing. Often, children will just write down everything they know about a topic; the text will lack structure and the key language features will be missing. The alternative is often that children will start quite well, but quickly regress and end up writing a narrative, i.e going back to the type of writing that they have experienced the most.

Subject knowledge

The second key reason that children often struggle with non-fiction writing is because of **limited subject knowledge**. It doesn't matter what the text type is, non-fiction writing is full of detail. It's not unusual in schools for teachers to link their non-fiction texts to their topic. For example, when studying the Egyptians we would ask the children to write a newspaper report on an Egyptian find. Yet, even when studying the topic, children often haven't yet internalised the required level of knowledge. They don't know enough about a topic, therefore they don't include enough detail.

Engagement

The third barrier relates to **engagement**. The danger with non-fiction texts is that often the traditional non-fiction topics just don't interest the children. Examples include instructions on how to make a cup of tea or a persuasive speech on wearing uniforms in school. It's dull. As adults, we would struggle to find inspiration to complete tasks, which we aren't interested in. How much harder, then, for children who are also being challenged to learn new skills at the same time?

Model Text

The final barrier is the **model text.** In my experience often teachers struggle to find appropriate model texts, pitched appropriately. If teachers don't have an effective model to use throughout the teaching sequence, the outcome for the children is naturally going to be ineffective too.

With the far greater emphasis on grammar, punctuation and spelling that has come with the implementation of the 2014 Primary National Curriculum, as well as its increased expectations of children's reading and writing development, the challenge for the twenty-first century teacher is to find a model text which not only engages the child, but also contains suitable language features, appropriate content and detail, and appropriately pitched vocabulary, grammar and punctuation.

This **Fun with Non-Fiction** book aims to address these barriers by providing modern primary teachers with a good range of high-quality texts pitched appropriately to meet the requirements of the National Curriculum for each year group. Each text has been written to engage, excite and inspire the children. The texts provide a professional model for the teacher to use to demonstrate 'what a good one looks like' and can be used as part of an effective teaching sequence. These fun texts have excited and inspired children and teachers across the UK and, if they're used in an effective and engaging teaching sequence, they really can transform children's non-fiction writing. You will note that there are seven different text types in this book. They should all be fairly self-explanatory, possibly aside from the distinction between 'argument' and 'discussion'. Historically, in primary schools, 'argument' has come to mean 'balanced argument', which has come to mean the same thing as 'discussion. However, we know that in the real world, when we 'argue' a point of view, it means that we are trying to put that point of view across. Therefore, in this book, we have taken 'argument' to have its real-world meaning. Thus, we have persuasive texts (completely one-sided, without recognition of another point of view), argument texts (explaining and then arguing against a point of view, in order to convince readers that the point of view is wrong) and discussion texts (balanced, stating both points of view fairly). Feel free to mix and match! There is nothing in the National Curriculum to prescribe what we might call the 'traditional' view of these terms, so let's reclaim them and bring them closer in line with what children will come across in the real world. After all, what is education, without real-life application?

Understanding The Path to Success

Before looking in any detail at the teaching sequence, it's important to understand the Path to Success.

A forward-thinking, innovative approach to teaching and learning in the twenty-first century classroom, the Path to Success can be applied across all subjects to support all primary schools in achieving outstanding results through engaged learning. The Path to Success is grounded in the latest educational research and first-hand experience of current teaching of real children in the primary classroom.

How is it different?

We are not advocating a scheme that primary schools, children and teachers have to follow in a particular order or predetermined way. In our experience, a predetermined scheme is unable to take account of all the various factors at play in any one classroom; including, but not limited to the skill set of the teacher and the ability range of the children.

The Path to Success is a circular methodology with talk, collaboration and active approaches at its heart. Its process can be applied across the curriculum, as the core techniques it embodies can be used to teach any skill or operation. Once teachers internalise this process, it has the potential to transform their practice and have a significant impact on standards.

WHAT DOES IT LOOK LIKE?

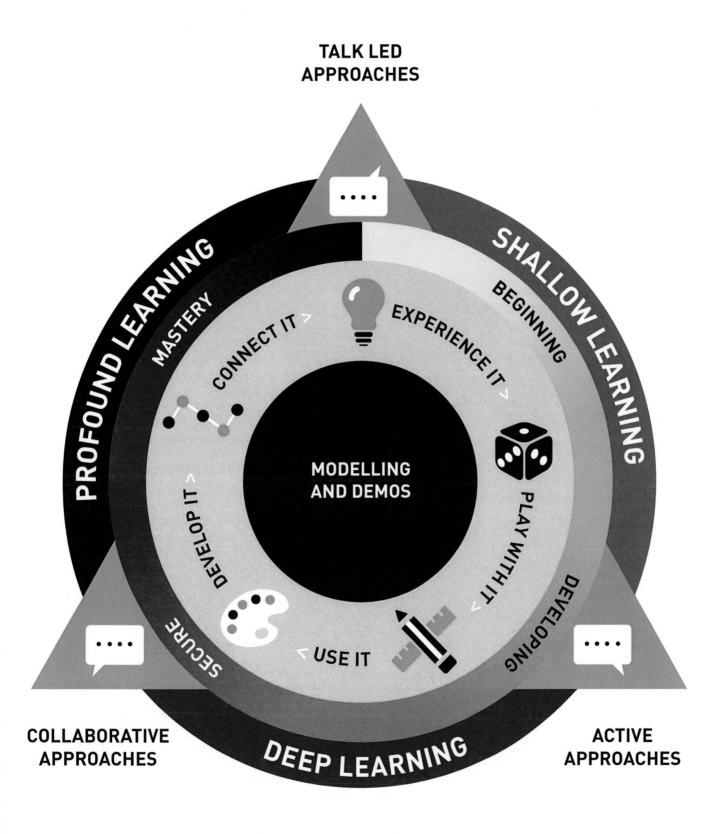

Teachers who use the Path to Success will develop and enrich children's ability to problem-solve, think creatively, improve their skills as learners and consequently make accelerated progress.

Stage 1: Experience it.

Children need rich experiences, which they can relate to, in order to support them in developing a particular skill set. For example, how can you expect a child to use a relative clause if they haven't experienced it in any type of meaningful context? The challenge for us as teachers is to find a way to replicate this meaningful experience and practical application in the classroom. Relative clauses will appear in a range of text types, but they frequently appear in newspaper reports, so providing children with a range of newspapers and getting children to experience finding relative clauses is a great starting point.

Stage 2: Play with it

This, in a sense, refers to the 'gamification' of learning. The power of playing short games to practise key skills on a daily basis should not be underestimated. Not only do they act as hooks to excite, engage and challenge the children but they also support children in developing fluency in a particular skill. By playing games with, for example, relative clauses (perhaps shifting them about in the sentence to see what different effects they can create), children are practising their procedural efficiency of using a relative clause in a newspaper report, while improving their conceptual understanding of why a relative clause could be used here and the impact it has on the audience and purpose.

Stage 3: Use it

Once children have experienced a particular skill and had an opportunity to play with it in order to fully assimilate the technique, they then move on to using it in context. Practical application in context is fundamental to successful outcomes for children.

"Tell me and I'll forget; show me and I may remember; involve me and I'll understand."

- Chinese proverb

Stage 4: Develop it

Children continue to develop the skill in context. It is absolutely crucial that all adults within the classroom, and within the school at large, position themselves alongside the children as learners, actively engaging in the learning process. High-quality modelling and demonstration should be underpinned by an active, talk-led, collaborative learning climate. It is in this sharing of the learning process that children find the inspiration to move from learners to teachers – if this move has been modelled by you, as the adult, they will follow your example! If a child can teach a particular skill, it means they must have learnt it and are more likely to remember it. As practitioners, we should be aiming to move all our children into becoming teachers. If a child can confidently demonstrate the level of understanding necessary for them to be able to explain and teach a concept, idea or approach to another child, then in doing so they are demonstrating that their initial learning has been internalised and embedded. By this stage they are demonstrating a move from shallow surface-level learning to deeper learning and understanding.

Step 5: Connect It

This refers to children making connections across the curriculum. With a deeper understanding, children will begin to make links and connections in terms of how they could apply the skill or concept they have just learnt across the curriculum and in the wider world. Making these connections and exploring possible connections moves the child from deep learning into profound learning; the learning becomes personal to the child, because he or she can see its application within his or her own world and apply it within his or her life. This is the point at which the learning becomes fully assimilated and stays with the child forever.

How to use the Model Texts within the Teaching Sequence

The teaching sequence for writing is underpinned by the Path to Success philosophy. Before starting any new text we suggest you carry out a formative assessment. Give your children 30-45 minutes and ask them to write an example of the text type you are about to study independently. This formative assessment is crucial for working out and assessing both your children's prior **experience** of the text type in question, but also the technical level of their ability in terms of language features, grammar etc.

Once you have marked this formative assessment, then consider your Hook, **Experience**, Context and Purpose. "Hook, Experience, Context and Purpose" is a refrain we use a lot when working with schools. We ask teachers to think back to the last unit or topic they taught and then to consider the four elements of the mantra:

- What was the hook you used to engage, inspire and excite your children?

- What experiences did children bring to the activity, or how were you able to replicate experiences to make the learning link to the real world?

- Did you choose a context that was relevant?

- Did all the children have a clear purpose for their learning, or was it simply 'complete the activities on page 10'?

Once you have done this, then choose a model text from the Fun with Non-Fiction range, or use one as a basis to create your own. Our models have been specially created to meet the requirements and expectations of the British National Curriculum. However, every class is different, and you may find that our texts give you the inspiration, structure and support to formulate your own.

Once you have chosen your model, the initial stage of the teaching sequence is read, analyse and discuss. At this stage, it is important to provide children with a range of non-fiction texts of the same genre as the model. These texts need to provide children with a rich experience of the text type in question. Children should be given opportunities to discuss the texts, ask questions and, if appropriate, retell the texts orally. Remember: 'talk is thought'. It is only when you talk the text through that you realise whether you have fully understood it. Talking allows us to develop our thinking, internally question our understanding and, ultimately, learn. Oral retelling is not only helpful for narrative texts, it is also very helpful for non-fiction texts. At Key Stage One, as with narrative, children should be learning non-fiction texts off by heart in order to fully assimilate their structures, language features and vocabulary. Once they have internalized these features, they will begin to be able to use them.

Children should also be encouraged to collaborate to gain an in-depth understanding of the text. They could complete sequencing activities; role-play the text; carry out analysis through identifying a list of key features; and annotate and highlight the text, identifying the structure, content, language features and grammar. Creating a classroom climate of collaboration is crucial for the long-term sustainability of learning. If we share a common purpose, we are incentivised to work together to develop our collective understanding. The barriers created by fear of personal failure are destroyed and we begin to recognise the power of our own contributions to the learning of the whole group. Not only does this create feelings of self-worth, excitement and engagement with the learning, but it also stimulates creativity and, in the discussion and development of ideas with peers, creates a deeper level of understanding.

At the same time as gaining this rich **experience**, children should be encouraged to develop their knowledge and confidence through fast-paced, short-burst games, which should happen on a daily basis across the curriculum. These games should be aimed at generating ideas, practising grammatically correct sentences and support the development of writing in a particular style or purpose. Children should be encouraged to **play with language and play with the text**. In the natural world, young animals learn through play. We are familiar with this as a concept with babies and toddlers; why, then, do we reject this as children begin to grow? When an idea or concept is made into a game – something which children recognise and respond to – children begin to engage with it and take ownership over it. 'Gamifying' learning allows children to generate ideas for themselves, cultivate their creativity, and lay the foundations for fluent learning.

Once the children have experience of the text and confidence to both generate ideas and manipulate language for effect, as teachers we then need to allow children opportunities to use these skills for a purpose. A great tool for planning is chunking. Chunking grids are modelled in this book on page 57, but, in effect, the aim is that children use chunking to identify and record the

structure, content and language features of their model text, as well as reflect on the purpose and effect of the text on the reader. Through constant repetition, children will learn to chunk the text quickly, and, as such, develop the ability to read as writers. They will be able to deduce and infer meaning from the text and will demonstrate how the author has had an effect on the reader. Of course, once the analysis has been done, children can use the same chunking grid as a planning tool. Your lower ability children will use the initial analysis as a form of scaffolding, while your more able children will increasingly draw on and use techniques and language from the rich experiences they have gained from texts to which they have previously been exposed.

With an effective plan, children will then be able to use this to inform the creation of their own non-fiction text. My suggestion would be to do one paragraph a day, so that by the end of the week every child has a complete non-fiction text. Teachers and TAs should engage in high quality shared writing on a daily basis. Children should be encouraged to **draft, redraft and edit and improve** and this should be modelled.

Once a child is able to analyse, plan and write their own text it is important to give them opportunities **to teach others**. It could be that they teach a teddy, an object, a friend or even an adult. Getting children to teach is a powerful tool for enabling deeper learning. You can't teach a skill unless you have fully grasped it. Teaching allows us to explain our thought process, demonstrate our understanding and make sense of our thinking. It gives us an opportunity to be an expert and embed and enrich our ideas. Teaching a skill makes it real, commits it to memory and enables us to then have the confidence to make **connections** and use the knowledge in a range of contexts.

With non-fiction, once a child is fully confident with a particular text type, they will then apply their knowledge across the curriculum and beyond. Here, they are able to demonstrate profound learning, and **unconscious competence**. They know how to apply and use both the text type and features without thinking about it. In effect they are able to demonstrate **mastery**. As teachers it's never been more important to allow children to have opportunities to write and apply skills across the curriculum and in a range of contexts. Make non-fiction fun, use the models, follow the Path to Success and enable your children to access a world of writing opportunities beyond their imagination.

David Maytham, 2015

PERSUASIVE TEXTS

What is a persuasive text?

When you persuade, you are trying to convince someone that your point of view is the correct one. This might be just because the writer wants the reader to agree with that point of view. It might be because the writer wants the reader to do something. Whatever the reason, a persuasive text is always completely one-sided and should not allow room for an alternative point of view. Persuasive texts are fun to write, because they are so one-sided. You can really have fun with them, asking the children to persuade the headteacher that they should all be allowed to have cake for lunch, or days off for their birthdays, or hot air balloons to transport them to and from school trips.

At upper Key Stage Two, to create a higher level of challenge, why not ask the children to persuade the class of an opinion that they do not actually hold? Ask them to persuade the class that their homework should be trebled (it's for their own good!), or that children are horrible and adults are the best, or that Christmas should be cancelled, because it's too expensive. Whatever the subject, have fun with it. The skills are the same, whether it's dull or exciting, and it will be remembered for a lot longer if children enjoy themselves.

Types of text that lend themselves well to persuasion: leaflets, speeches, blogs, letters, posters, emails, adverts, scripts.

Features of persuasive writing[1]

- All persuasive texts should start with a clear introduction, setting out the writer's point of view.

- There could be past, present and future tenses used – there should ideally be a mixture (Years ago, our parents were allowed to eat lots of delicious cake for their school dinners. These days, it is all about 'healthy eating' and 'keeping fit'. What will future generations think, when they look back at us and realise that children in the twenty-first century were denied their fundamental human right to eat as much cake as they want?).

- Imperative verbs are useful, to exhort the reader to consider the writer's opinion (Imagine the outcry if adults were denied cake!).

- A variety of conjunctions will be necessary, to show cause, exemplification and summary (therefore, consequently, for example, thus, in conclusion, in summary).

- Rhetorical questions, to get the reader considering the writer's point of view, are very helpful.

- Hyperbole (exaggerated language for effect) is vital.

- Constant repetition, both of the main point and of salient details throughout, will help to etch the point of the writing on the reader's mind, as will patterns of three.

- Emotive language plays on the reader's feelings to make them more likely to agree.

- It is vital, also, that lots of facts and statistics are used, to make the writer seem more believable. Sometimes, opinions can be presented as though they are facts, and this is a great technique in persuasive writing (Cake is one of the most important types of food there is...).

- There are different levels of formality necessary in persuasive writing, dependent on the text type, but at upper Key Stage Two, children should be encouraged to experiment with increasing levels of formality, in order to stretch themselves and include more complex vocabulary, sentences structures and grammar.

[1] Naturally, this is an exhaustive list. Class teachers must use their judgement as to which are age-appropriate and ability-appropriate for their children.

WHY MY CLASS IS THE BEST!

Hello. I would like to tell you why my class is the best. The other classes are good, but we are the best. Do you want to know why? There are lots of reasons.

One reason is that the children in my class are very kind. We play well with each other. We always share. We never hit or call each other nasty names. That is one reason why we are the best.

Next, I will talk about playtime. The children in my class are very good at playtime. We do not make lots of noise. We are not silly. We play with our friends sensibly, so we can all have lots of fun.

You can see that there are lots of reasons why my class is the best!

Why Jack Should Be Kinder

First, when I read Jack and the Beanstalk, I felt sorry for Jack's mother. She is poor and Jack is not very helpful to her. Jack should be kinder.

Soon, Jack seemed even nastier. He stole from the giant! It was unkind of Jack to take things that belonged to someone else. Jack should be kinder.

After that, the story gets even worse. Jack chopped down the beanstalk while the giant was still on it. Poor giant! Jack should be kinder.

In the end, Jack is happy, but the giant is not. Jack has been very selfish. He only thinks about himself and not about the sad giant or his poor mother. Jack should be kinder to the giant and his mother.

WHY WE SHOULD TURN OUR SCHOOL INTO A CASTLE!

Hello everyone. Today, I would like to tell you why I think we should turn our school into a castle. All teachers want their children to enjoy coming to school. They plan interesting lessons and are always witty! There is only one thing that teachers could change to make school better for their classes. That is the building. School buildings are a bit square and flat and not very interesting. The best way to make a school look more exciting is to make it into a castle! Children love castles, because they are strange and spooky. Don't you think that would be exciting in our school?

It would be easy to turn our school into a castle. The only big things we would need would be some turrets and a moat. The children could easily make the turrets in their lessons. It wouldn't be difficult to dig a moat either. We could make it part of PE lessons, because it would give the children lots of exercise. I think it would be fun too!

A castle would also be very safe, because castles were built to be safe! Children would very quickly get used to the new layout of the school and it would be fun to play with the moat and drawbridge at playtime.

As you can see, turning a school into a castle would be very safe, fun and easy. It would make everyone in the school happier and our school would be the most unusual and interesting one in the whole country!

My School,
My Town,
My County,
MY1 0SC.

Dear Father Christmas,

How are you? I do hope you are feeling well and looking forward to delivering all the children's gifts this year. I know you get lots of letters all year from children asking for different toys and presents, so I will get straight to the point. This year, I don't think you should bring presents to all the children in the world by sleigh.

Santa, it's the twenty-first century. Nobody uses sleighs any more. They are very old-fashioned and it must be a struggle for you to fit all the presents in, as the world's population has increased a lot since you first started making your deliveries. Although it is nice to keep up old traditions, it isn't sensible to ignore the benefits of the modern world.

Why not invest in a bright, shiny, fresh ship? There are some very large cruise ships these days. These would have space for plenty of gifts and would travel very calmly through the sky, without any jerky movements. Do reindeer travel smoothly? I would guess not. You deserve a nice, gentle journey at your age.

The night of Christmas Eve must be very tiring for you. I'm sure it would be much better if you could finish a little earlier. With a newer and more efficient vehicle, I am sure that you could easily speed up your trip. You don't need to keep using your old, slow, bumpy sleigh.

I hope I have shown you that there are other options for your travel needs. Please do consider them. I think it would be much better for your health.

Good luck on December 24th!

Yours sincerely,

Anne Adolescent

Anne Adolescent

WHY WE SHOULD RECYCLE MORE

Good afternoon. I am here today to talk to you about recycling. It is an issue which affects everyone in the world. However, there are a lot of people in this country who do not bother with recycling. They don't see why it's important. They don't see how it affects them. They don't understand why they should bother. That is why I am here today, to show you exactly why it is important, exactly how it affects you and exactly why you should bother to recycle.

The first point I would like to talk about is why recycling is important. Did you know that we only recycle around 17% of our products in the UK? When you compare this to other countries, who recycle over 50%, it doesn't look good. Most families throw away 40kg of plastic rubbish every year. That's the same weight as an average four-year-old child! This is really bad, because plastic can take up to 500 years to decompose. How horrible is that? This just goes to show how important it is to recycle.

You may be wondering exactly how this affects you personally. In this country, we waste thirty-six million pounds every year. That is the cost of all the aluminium which we throw away instead of recycling. What a silly thing to do! It's throwing money down the drain! That money could be spent on hospitals, schools or youth centres. Instead, it is wasted by people who think recycling doesn't affect them. If you think that, you're wrong.

Hopefully, I have already shown you why you should bother recycling. However, I have one more point to make. Recycling is easy! How hard is it to put a can in a different bin? It's not hard at all. So if it's going to save the environment, save the country money and isn't going to make your life any more difficult, why not do it? Your children will thank you for it, because you're making the world a better place for them.

In conclusion, I'd like to thank you for listening to me. I hope you agree that not recycling is simply wasteful, ignorant and lazy. Now you have the facts, you can begin to make changes to the way you treat your rubbish. Don't forget, around 16% of your money goes on packaging. So if you're throwing it away, you're just wasting that money. Do yourself a favour: recycle.

In the next General Election:
WHY YOU SHOULD VOTE FOR CANDI DATE!
January 2020
A member of the Chocolate-Eating Party

POLICIES

EMPLOYMENT

When I am appointed Prime Minister (as I am certain I shall be), I shall immediately set about creating new jobs in the chocolate industry. It is absolutely criminal that there are so few chocolate factories in this great country of ours. I shall rectify this error as soon as I am given the power to do so.

AGRICULTURE

The amount of milk and milk products the extra factories will require will be astonishing. Therefore, it is clear that farming in this country will be given a boost. This will, naturally, also create more jobs, thus proving what a stroke of genius it really is to open the new factories.

EDUCATION

There are few changes that need to be made to education in this country. After all, I, myself, am a product of the British educational system and I'm pretty awesome. The primary change that will need to be introduced is a History of Chocolate module in every year group.

IN CONCLUSION...

I think your way forward is plain. Run – don't walk – to that ballot box on the day of the election and cast your vote for Candi Date: the only sensible option.

WHY I DESERVE YOUR VOTE

MY QUALITIES

Even when I was a child, it was obvious to everyone who knew me that I was destined for greatness. I was more devoted to chocolate than any child had ever been. This complete loyalty is something I could bring to the role of Prime Minister. I would devote myself entirely to my country's needs (mostly the need to produce more chocolate, which is something I will talk about later, but I do understand that there might be a few other things too).

My intelligence, originality and flexibility are also assets that I would bring to the role of Prime Minister. Hopefully, my intelligence is obvious. If you need proof, I would ask you only one question: has anybody else ever formed a Chocolate-Eating political party? Exactly. I saw a gap in the government and I have filled it. With chocolate. This also demonstrates my originality. I have absolutely no political experience, yet I had the original notion to go into politics anyway, with an original campaign, focused on the most important area of people's lives: chocolate.

Lastly, my flexibility can clearly be seen by the fact that I can fit a whole Twix in my mouth. Both fingers. Now that's flexible.

MY BACKGROUND

I was born. I grew up. What more do you need to know? Where I have come from is unimportant. What is important is where I am going: 10 Downing Street. This is where I belong. If you need further proof, come along to Buckingham Palace on 12th February to see me showing off my world-famous skill at 'downing' hot chocolate. The clue is in the name, people!

FOR ANY QUESTIONS, PLEASE WRITE TO:

Coco Krisp,
3 Milky Lane,
Beanton.

VOTE CANDI DATE!
THE ONLY SENSIBLE OPTION.

Thanks to:
Willy Wonka and Lord Scrumptious.

WHY YOU SHOULD VISIT OXFORD

Of all the cities in all the worlds in all the universes there have ever been, there is only one whose beauty, intrigue and historical charm has never been exaggerated: Oxford. If you never visit anywhere else in the entire course of your life; if you never set foot outside of your own front door for any other purpose; if you live life blindfolded, deafened and entirely switched off to every other place; still, you simply must visit Oxford.

It is almost impossible to think of where to begin when enumerating the reasons for Oxford's appeal. However, if I were really pressed, I would say that the most appealing aspect of it is its architecture. Nowhere has there been such a creative explosion of building sculpture than in Oxford. The ancient sits alongside the brand new in perfect harmony. The quaint and delightful complements the modern and impressive in an idyllic manner. There is simply nothing more fascinating than a trip through the little back lanes of this mesmerizing city, soaking in the architectural culture through your awestruck eyeballs. And that's not all

Who doesn't love to cycle? It is a well-known fact that cycling is one of the best forms of exercise there is and in Oxford you can enjoy this relaxing, energizing, invigorating activity in complete safety. Due to the fact that the city is totally pedestrianised, there is no need to worry at all about the noisy, smelly, perilous motorised vehicles that blight practically every other city in existence. What a novelty! To explore without fear of loss of life or limb: what could be finer?

Well, I'll tell you something finer! Even finer and more impressive than this is the huge and fantastic range of fine dining opportunities available in Oxford. You cannot walk more than a few paces before stumbling across one of the city's fabulous restaurants, cafes or bistros. Whatever cuisine appeals most to you, you need look no further – it's here! From melt-in-the-mouth morning munchies to delicious Michelin-star, three-course dining, there is nothing Oxford is lacking.

Last in my list, but certainly not least, are the historical opportunities you are exposed to in Oxford. The university is wonderfully interesting to visit, as are the sites of the filming of the Harry Potter films. Indeed, were I to list the number of incredible places there are to visit, I would soon run out of space, so I shall content myself with saying: there is nowhere in Oxford that you shouldn't visit, so make it a long visit and make it soon!

In conclusion, it would be madness to miss Oxford. Madness. Book your trip today!

ARGUMENT TEXTS

What is an argument?

The Oxford English Dictionary has a variety of definitions of the verb 'argue'. In essence, however, it appears to boil down to this: to argue is to put across one's point of view in the face of opposition. This is probably how we use it most often in everyday life. Therefore, a written argument needs to do just this – it needs to put across a point of view in the face of opposition. To do this, a piece of argument writing needs to:

- state the case for the opposing view

- clearly refute that view

Take a look at the arguments in this section for some examples.

In reception and Key Stage One, it is advisable to keep things very simple, as showing two different points of view has the potential to become complicated. Children can write down an idea or perhaps a couple of ideas, show why they disagree with them and then conclude their writing. However, by the time they reach Year Six, they should be at least attempting to follow an ABAB structure where A is a paragraph which sets out one point for the opposing view and B is their personal opinion, refuting A's claim. For example:

A: Some people say that foxhunting is necessary to keep fox populations under control.

B: However, this is clearly ridiculous; since when did we become the 'fox police'? We have no right to control the population of another species.

A: Another point pro-foxhunters make is that hunting is fun. Lots of people really enjoy it.

B: On the other hand, people probably enjoyed having slaves to wait on them, but that doesn't make slavery morally right, so that's another ridiculous point.

In real life, this is how arguments work. Whether it is in conversation with peers, taking part in a formal debate or defending an idea in the boardroom, this is how we expect to argue in adult life: not by ignoring opposition, but by methodically taking apart the opposition in order to demonstrate its flaws. The degree to which the writer is biased can vary; in some cases the writer can show that he or she believes the opposing view to be worthy of some respect, but there should always be a judgement at the end and the opposing view should always be shown to be invalid.

Types of text that lend themselves well to arguments: leaflets, speeches, scripts, letters, emails.

Features of argument writing[1]

- Short introduction which sets out writer's view.

- ABAB structure (where age-appropriate).

- Lots of contrast conjunctions (e.g. on the other hand, however, nevertheless).

- Writer's view made clear with personal pronouns.

- A combination of past, present and future tenses (In the olden days, foxhunting was seen as a great sport/How will future generations view us, when they look back at this violent pastime?).

- Rhetorical questions.

- Hyperbole (exaggerated language for effect).

- Comparative and superlative adjectives (worst, most ridiculous).

- Statistics and other facts (90% of Britons believe that foxhunting is wrong).

- Repetition (particularly of the main thrust of the argument, in order to remind the reader of the writer's point of view).

- Emotive language and imperatives (Imagine the defenceless little fox cowering in fear...).

- Patterns of three and sentences of three when age appropriate (It is clear that foxhunting is part of an old-fashioned way of life; it promotes violence and aggression; and it is inescapably elitist).

- Opposing view made clear with impersonal pronouns and/or passive voice (where age-appropriate) e.g. 'It has been stated that...' 'Some people think...'.

- Clear choice of verbs for each paragraph (e.g. tenuous verbs such as 'claim', 'think', 'believe' for the opposing view, contrasted with 'know', 'demonstrate' for the writer's view).

- Strong adverbs to support writer's view (e.g. clearly, obviously).

- Brief conclusion, assuming that reader is now completely on writer's side and summarising main point.

[1] Naturally, this is an exhaustive list. Class teachers must use their judgement as to which are age-appropriate and ability-appropriate for their children.

Why chocolate is better than sweets.

Chocolate and sweets are both really nice. Some people prefer sweets. Some people prefer chocolate. I think chocolate is the best.

People who like sweets say that they are colourful and you get lots of them. They also say that sweets are smaller than chocolate so they are healthier. That is why people think that they are better than chocolate.

I don't agree. Having lots of different sweets is not good. Some might be horrible. Chocolate is the same all over. Chocolate and sweets both have lots of sugar in them, but chocolate has milk in it too. Milk is good for you! Chocolate has good things in it as well as bad things. That is why I think that chocolate is better than sweets.

I think it is very clear that chocolate is the best!

WHY FAIRIES SHOULD COME AND LIVE IN OUR SCHOOL

Good morning. I am here today to talk to you about fairies. Fairies are little magical creatures. They live inside people's houses and other buildings. Some people think it would be good if they lived in our school, but some people don't. I think it would be good and I will tell you why.

First, some people think that fairies are pests. They worry that the fairies would make a mess and maybe even be smelly. Other people argue that having lots of people around would scare the poor little fairies. Fairies are very shy and don't like to be seen.

I don't agree with this. Actually, fairies are very clean and tidy. Fairies are much tidier than most people. It is true that fairies are very shy, but they usually only come out at night. There is nobody in schools at night. This would be perfect for the fairies. They could play quite happily and not worry about a person seeing them.

I think it is clear that a school is the perfect place for a fairy to live. It would be quiet for them and they would not make a mess. We should ask them to move in tomorrow! Thank you for listening.

Why we should be kinder to spiders?

Lots of people are scared of spiders and many more people just don't like them. Most people think that they are pests. Because spiders are small and get into our houses, we often squash them. I think we should be kinder to spiders and I will tell you why they are not pests.

First, people call spiders pests, but pests are useless. Spiders are not useless. If there were no spiders, our houses would be full of flies, mosquitoes and wasps. Those creatures really are pests. Spiders trap these pests in their webs and stop them invading our homes. We should thank the spiders for that! As well as stopping bugs bothering us, spiders also stop them from eating all the crops that we need to make food. If we had no spiders, we would have no food and insects would pester us all the time. We should say thank you to the spiders!

People also complain about the webs that spiders build. They say that the webs are dirty and horrible to touch and make everything look messy. This may be true, but did you know that they are also incredibly useful? Spiders spin silk to make their webs. People use that silk for all sorts of things. Spider silk has been used to make fishing nets, rain hats and even clothes! That doesn't sound dirty or messy to me!

I think it is plain to see that spiders are not pests. They are very useful and helpful creatures. If we didn't have them, we would have no food. If we didn't have them, we would have no spider silk to make things with. If we didn't have them, we would have insects crawling all over our homes. We should be grateful for spiders and we should be much kinder to them.

WHY MAKING UP STORIES IS THE BEST GAME EVER!

Whenever I am bored and I can't think of anything to do, I always fall back on my favourite game of making up stories. Lots of people think that making up stories is a silly game. They can't understand why I do it. Let me explain it to you.

Although I know that many people see making up stories as hard work, it really isn't hard at all. I'm only doing it for myself, so it doesn't have to be a super story. Unless you want to make it long and complicated, there is no need to spend ages on it. Making up stories about why the cat has ginger fur or inventing a pretend subject for the people opposite me in the café to be talking about is funny! There are so many silly, funny and interesting things to think about that it's really not hard work at all.

However, some people might think that making up stories is pointless. After all, there are thousands of stories already out there. You could just read a great book or watch a DVD or TV programme. Why re-invent the wheel? This is a ridiculous thing to say! What if Francesca Simon had thought that? She would never have created Horrid Henry! What if Roald Dahl had thought that? He would never have written Matilda or Charlie and the Chocolate Factory! What if J. K. Rowling had thought that? She would never have written Harry Potter! Making up silly stories might seem a million miles away from writing a whole book, but it's exercise for your mind. If you want to run a marathon, you don't just run twenty-six miles on your first day, do you? You start small. This is no different.

It is obvious from what I have said that making up stories is the greatest game in the world. There is no better way to prepare yourself for being a wonderful writer in the future and it's really not difficult. Why not try it?

WHY SHOULDN'T SELL SWEETS TO CHILDREN

I'M SURE THAT A LOT OF PEOPLE WOULD BE VERY UPSET IF SHOPS STOPPED SELLING SWEETS TO CHILDREN. HOWEVER, I BELIEVE THAT IT IS VERY IMPORTANT THAT SHOPS STOP THIS TERRIBLE HABIT IMMEDIATELY. THEY ARE IRRESPONSIBLE TO EVEN THINK ABOUT DOING IT AND I SHALL TELL YOU WHY.

Some people believe that children should be allowed to spend their pocket money on whatever they like. They say that this allows children to understand what it will be like when they grow up and have to manage their own money. However, I disagree. Everyone knows that children can't look after anything. Children are not clever enough to understand things and allowing them to buy their own sweets is just the first step in allowing them to think and have opinions. Children shouldn't be allowed to have opinions about anything! They might start actually talking to grown-ups. How awful! This is clearly not something we can allow. Therefore, children should not be allowed to buy sweets.

On the other hand, some people would argue that children should be allowed a treat once in a while. They work hard at school and help their parents in the house, so they should have something nice sometimes. This is outrageous. Children should never be allowed nice things. Children are loud and rude and smelly. Allowing them nice things will only encourage them to be louder and ruder and smellier. This does not sound like a good idea to me! This is further proof that children should not be allowed to buy sweets.

Another point that some people make on the topic of why children should be allowed to buy sweets is that children need snacks to keep them full of energy. Children need lots of energy to help them grow and make sure they are able to run around and play. Sweets are one way to get this energy. I'm sure you can imagine what I think about this! Ridiculous! Although children should be made to grow up as quickly as possible to get rid of all that horrible smallness, giving them energy is the last thing we need. Children should be kept as quiet as possible. There are hundreds of things they could eat to make them grow, but keep them quiet. The best sort of food to give them would be something like raisins or peanuts or anything that can be thrown through the bars of their cages easily.

In conclusion, I think it is obvious that sweetshop owners should all be arrested immediately. Children should not be allowed to buy sweets, because it will encourage them to have opinions, make them louder and ruder, and give them far too much energy.

WHY SNOW WHITE SHOULD NOT MARRY THE PRINCE

Good morning. Thank you for coming today. I am here to talk to you about a topic I feel very strongly about. Of all the fairy tales in the world, Snow White is one of the most famous. However, I strongly disagree with her actions in the story. Therefore, I will show you why I think that Snow White should not marry the prince.

Most people think that Snow White should marry the prince. They say that it is her destiny, because only true love's kiss could wake her from her sleep. The prince's kiss woke her, therefore it must be true love. However, this is the daftest thing I have ever heard. First, isn't it slightly creepy that this guy likes to go around kissing random women while they sleep? Secondly, it could easily be a coincidence. It seems like an unlikely story that only true love's kiss could wake the sleeping princess. I wouldn't be at all surprised if the prince just made that bit up to explain his bad behaviour. After all, what's the worst that could happen? The prince could just say, "Oh, she didn't wake up. I guess it's not true love after all. Not to worry. Plenty more fish in the sea. Let's head off to the palace then." I bet he was really surprised when it actually worked! It's much more likely that Snow White had a piece of the poisoned apple stuck in her throat and his kiss moved it. It's definitely not destiny at work here. Accidental first aid, maybe. Destiny, no.

Another reason that people could give for Snow White and the prince getting married is that she has nowhere else to go. After all, her stepmother is trying to kill her and she can't go back to her home. However, again, this is daft. Why can't she stay with the dwarfs? They seem to really like her and she does their housework for free, so it's only fair that she gets to live there for free. It would be the easiest

solution. If the prince likes her, he can come and visit and get to know her. Then, if they decide that they really do love one another, they can consider marriage. Basing a marriage on a thirty second kiss, during which one of them was asleep, is not the healthiest start to a relationship!

The only other argument that I can think of as to why Snow White ought to marry the prince is the simple fact that he is a prince. He's rich, powerful and handsome. She's a homeless princess with a homicidal stepmother. It's a match made in heaven, isn't it? I do see that point of view. However, I would argue that this is not a reason to marry. Make friends with the prince, by all means. If he is a kind person, he might be able to use his power as a prince to do something about the homicidal stepmother. However, anyone who will only stop you being poisoned if you will marry them is a blackmailing brute and Snow White can definitely do better for herself. Also, she really needs to stand up for herself and not rely on a man to do it for her. She needs to have a word with her stepmother, woman to woman and come to some sort of resolution together.

I think it is clear that Snow White really ought not to marry the prince. Not only does he come across as a little bit creepy and, possibly, a blackmailer, but she really ought to be a bit stronger and sort her own problems out. Relying on true love to rescue you is a bit of a wishy-washy way to live. She needs to take control of her life, have a word with her stepmother and tell the prince, firmly, that she is happy to be his friend, as long as he visits her in the dwarfs' cottage, where she has independence, a lovely group of friends and her own job. Thank you for listening.

WERE SHAKESPEARE'S PLAYS REALLY WRITTEN BY HIM?

Good afternoon. Thank you for joining me at our Shakespeare Conference today. For centuries now, people have wondered whether the group of plays we usually call "Shakespeare's" were actually written by Shakespeare – or even by just one person at all. Several names have been put forward and there are many people out there who refuse to accept that a humble country boy from Stratford-upon-Avon could ever really have written thirty-seven incredible plays, which have moved us to tears, laughter and terror for over four hundred years. In this speech, I will attempt to untangle this knotty problem.

One of the first things anti-Stratfordians (people who don't believe that Shakespeare really wrote all those plays) refer to is almost always the sheer number of Shakespeare's plays. Thirty-seven plays in twenty-three years! How could that possibly be the work of one man? This amounts to more than one full play per year. At the same time, Shakespeare would have been acting in several of them at a time, as well as editing them (as he must have done) on an almost daily basis. This seems almost impossible. Considering how long some of the plays are – over 4000 lines in Hamlet alone – it gets more and more unlikely. When we look at the number of plays written by other writers in Shakespeare's day, such as Christopher Marlowe (seven plays) or Ben Jonson (twenty plays written in over forty years), it seems an enormous number. This is what leads some people to imagine that perhaps "Shakespeare" was actually a group of writers, who may have used the name of the actor, William Shakespeare, because they didn't want anyone to know who they were.

On the other hand, it is clear to see that not all writers write at the same rate. If we look at more modern writers, it is easy to see the difference between, for example, Harper Lee (writer of only two books, published 55 years apart) and John Grisham (who has written and published around thirty-five books in twenty-six years). Every writer is different, just as every person is different. As to whether one person could have written as much as Shakespeare did back in the olden days, Thomas Middleton, who lived around the same time, wrote much more than thirty-seven plays, along with poetry and other writing too. In case you're wondering, nobody has ever questioned whether Middleton really wrote his plays! It seems clear that trying to argue that a writer couldn't have written this number of plays is a bit daft...

The second thing that anti-Stradfordians talk about is Shakespeare's education. How could a poor, uneducated country boy become one of the most celebrated playwrights of all time? For an ignorant boy from the countryside to, all of a sudden, become fairly rich, very famous and end up performing plays in front of the Queen seems an unlikely story. For him to be credited with writing the plays that caused this huge promotion seems pretty much impossible. Even an admirer, Ben Jonson, admitted that Shakespeare had "small Latin and less Greek". This implies that he was not well educated, as education in Shakespeare's day usually meant lots and lots of Latin and Greek. How could he possibly have written so much and so well with so little education? Several of his plays make references to Latin and Greek writers also – how do we explain this? Simple. He cannot have written the plays.

However, this is not entirely accurate. Shakespeare was not just a 'country boy'. His father, John, was well off. In fact, he was the Mayor of Stratford when William was a child. He had a large (and expensive) house and would have easily been able to afford to send his children to school. John was a middle-class businessman, not a poor working-class labourer. Thus, it is likely that his son would have had the education necessary to write and to be able to make Latin and Greek references. Additionally, when you look more closely at his plays, they are full of country sayings. There are literally hundreds of examples where Shakespeare has used words and phrases that originated from the countryside – just like he did. Yes, it's a fantastic success story, but it's not an unbelievable one.

The final objection made by anti-Stratfordians is that there are very few documents that prove that Shakespeare wrote his plays. There are hardly any documents that prove that Shakespeare owned the plays. He didn't refer to them in his will. Copies of the plays weren't found in his house in Stratford. We know he had a family in Stratford, so he must have spent at least some time there; it seems odd that his two worlds never connected. Where is the proof?

The answer to this is: on the front covers of the plays! When Shakespeare's plays were first printed (in what is called the First Folio), they had his name on them. Plays in Elizabethan times were very rarely printed. When they were, they often had no name on them. The fact that Shakespeare's name was on his printed plays implies that he was quite a famous playwright by this point. People wanted the plays because they had heard of him and knew he was good! Really, the question we should be asking is: where is the proof that anyone else wrote the plays? The answer? There is none. No shred of evidence at all points to anybody else at in the world as the author of Shakespeare's plays. It seems clear, then, that this is not a very valid argument either.

In summary then, it seems to be clear that there is really very little cause to doubt that Shakespeare was the writer of the plays. Though it is amazing that one person should have created so many wonderful works, there is no evidence that it is impossible. While we can wonder about the quality of Shakespeare's education, there is no proof that there was anything wrong with it. And finally, while there is no historical document that says "Hi, it's me, Shakespeare, I definitely wrote all these plays", it seems crazy to decide that the lack of this document means that he didn't! In summary, I think it is clear that Shakespeare was indeed the wonderful writer most of us have always taken him to be. Thank you for listening and do have a safe journey home.

DISCUSSION TEXTS

What is a discussion?

Similarly to 'argument', 'discussion' is a word we use frequently in everyday life. We know what it means, yet when we teach it, we often teach something different to what our common sense tells us. In everyday life, to 'discuss' something means to consider a complex issue from both sides. We often don't even come to any real conclusion – the discussion is just a chance for both sides to state their case. Therefore, when we are teaching children to write a discussion text, that is exactly what we should be expecting of them. They should state the case for both sides, equally and without bias. In reception and Key Stage One, it is perfectly acceptable for children to state the case for one side first, then the other, then conclude their writing. By the end of Key Stage Two, it would be more appropriate for children to be writing in an ABAB structure to more accurately represent a real-life discussion or debate, like so:

A: Some people think that geese are scary birds and they should all be locked up.

B: However, it could be seen as unfair to punish the geese for the way people view them – it's not their fault.

A: On the other hand, others would argue that they can be quite vicious. There were several goose attacks last year.

B: Nevertheless, it is only fair to remember that they are wild animals. Some would say that we ought to just stay away from them if we don't want to be attacked.

Discussions should leave it open to the reader to decide what side they are on. The writer may have his or her own opinion, but it should not be expressed within their writing.

Types of writing which lend themselves well to discussions include: letters, emails, scripts and newspaper editorials.

Features of discussion writing[1]

- Brief introduction to present topic. At Key Stage One, this can be just a sentence, e.g. Today, we are going to talk about whether geese should all be locked up. At Key Stage Two, a little more information should be expected, regarding the two sides that will be presented.

- Primarily present tense should be used.

- Rhetorical questions.

- Lots of comparative and additional conjunctions, e.g. on the other hand, conversely, alternatively, that said, however, nevertheless, additionally, also.

- Lots of impersonal, third person phrases, such as 'some people believe that', 'it could be argued that', 'it appears that', 'it has been said that'.

- Equal numbers of points for and against.

- Formal tone to emphasise the writer's objectivity.

- A clear conclusive conjunction for the final paragraph.

- Conclusion should summarise the main issue, but not give a judgement.

[1] Naturally, this is an exhaustive list. Class teachers must use their judgement as to which are age-appropriate and ability-appropriate for their children.

IS SUMMER BETTER THAN WINTER?

Some people really like hot weather and some people really like cold weather. It is not easy to choose between summer and winter.

There are lots of good things about summer. It is nice when it's warm and sunny. It is nice to go to the beach and play outside. It is nice when there are flowers everywhere. That is why summer is good.

Sometimes summer is bad. It is not nice to get sunburnt. It is not nice when there are wasps and insects everywhere. It is not nice for some people get hayfever and sneeze. That is what is bad about summer.

There are lots of good things about winter. It is nice when it snows and we can build snowmen. It is nice to see the trees looking pretty in the frost. It is nice when you snuggle under a blanket and drink hot chocolate to feel cosy. That is why winter is good.

Sometimes winter is bad. It is not nice to get cold and wet. It is not nice when you feel shivery at night and you can't sleep. It is not nice when the days are dark and very short. That is what is bad about winter.

I think winter and summer both have good and bad points. Which do you think is best?

Should trolls be banned?

Many people are afraid of trolls. They say that trolls should be banned from coming into our towns and cities. It is an interesting idea, but there are always two sides to everything.

One reason that it would be good if trolls were banned is that they are very smelly. It's not much fun having to live near stinky old troll feet! That is a good reason to ban them.

Sometimes trolls eat cats and dogs. It would be terrible if a troll was allowed to live next door to you and then it ate your pet cat! That is a good reason to ban them.

Trolls are quite funny though. They are very good at telling jokes and they make people laugh all the time. That is a good reason to keep them.

Trolls do keep gardens tidy as well. They can easily make anything grow with their special troll magic. That is a good reason to keep them.

It is plain to see that this is a difficult question. You will have to make up your own minds.

SHOULD THE SUMMER HOLIDAYS BE LONGER?

Good morning everyone. Thank you for coming.

I am here to discuss whether school holidays should be longer. This is an interesting question and I think there are good points to be made for both sides.

Some people would say that six weeks is not long enough to spend with your family. We spend lots of time at school with our teachers, but what about our brothers, sisters or parents? It is nice for children to spend time with their families too.

Another reason that people say that the summer holidays are not long enough is that they fly by so quickly. A lot of people go away on holiday during the summer holidays. If you don't go away, you often go out to different places than usual. It is difficult to fit in all the lovely things you want to do in just six weeks.

Others disagree. They say that six weeks is a very long time to be away from your friends. Everyone is busy in the summer holidays, so it is difficult to arrange play dates with your friends. You will probably miss your friends a lot and look forward to coming back to school to see them.

Others argue that spending too much time out in the sun is not good for children. They worry about us getting sunburnt or getting sunstroke. It would be horrible to end up with red, sore skin. You could say that school is helpful, because at school we have time indoors, so we don't get too much sun.

You can see that there are good reasons for making the holidays longer, but there are also good reasons for keeping them the same. You will have to make up your own minds! Thank you very much for listening to my speech. I hope you enjoyed it.

Should magic be taught in primary schools?

Although there have been many stories about magic, nobody has ever considered teaching it to children in primary schools. It's great to teach it in certain selective secondary schools, but should primary school children have that opportunity too? It's an interesting question, so let's look at the arguments for and against.

One reason it is a good idea is that, if magic were to be taught to all primary school children, it would be easier to see who has magic powers. It might be that someone is a bit magical, but they have never tried to cast a spell and they don't know that they can. If everybody had lessons, magical children would be spotted earlier and they would be able to practise their skills. This is a good reason why magic should be taught in primary schools.

However, one reason it is a bad idea is that, if magic were to be taught to everyone, it would take up a lot of time in the school day. Magic is quite hard, so the lessons would have to be quite long. If lots of time is spent on one thing, there would be much less time to spend on things like reading and writing. It is more important for children to leave primary school able to read and write than for them to be able to cast a few spells. This is an important reason why magic should not be taught in primary schools.

On the other hand, magic is a very useful tool. If children could be taught how to do things with magic, they would be able to help out more at home. They could help their parents with the cooking and the cleaning and it would only take a few seconds to tidy their bedrooms. This would be a great time saver. It would also help children learn to take more responsibility, while still being safe and without taking lots of time. This is a good reason why magic should be taught in primary schools.

However, another reason it is a bad idea is that magic is quite dangerous. Before children are taught to cast spells, they really need to be a bit older. There are plenty of science experiments that children are not allowed to do until they reach secondary school. Older children are much more capable of taking sensible health and safety measures to stop their magic being too dangerous. Therefore, it can be argued that primary school children are simply too young to be taught magic. This is a good reason why magic should not be taught in primary schools.

All in all, I think this is a difficult question to answer. There are good arguments for and against. I will leave it to you to decide.

Should all wolves be locked up?

There has been a lot of discussion recently about the recent outbreak of bad behavior by wolves. Whether it is dressing up in order to dine on little girls or using their incredible lungs to blow innocent piggies' houses away, it is safe to say that there are some wolves who are really creating a terrible name for themselves. The question is, therefore, whether we ought to lock them all up to prevent this sort of thing happening in the future. That is what we need to discuss. I will set out the points for and against and we can consider each point of view.

The most obvious argument for locking them up is that they have proven themselves to be dangerous. Nibbling little girls and swallowing down old grannies is completely unacceptable. The wolf community needs to keep these bad wolves on a tighter leash and stop them causing such havoc. If one is dangerous, they all have the potential to be dangerous, so we should take action to prevent them eating us all. Who knows where it could lead? That is the first reason why we should lock them all up.

The most obvious argument for not locking them up is that the vast majority of them have done nothing wrong at all. We cannot punish the innocent for the sake of a tiny minority of wrongdoers. There are around 200,000 wolves living in the world today. We know of only two that have caused any trouble. It is true that the trouble they caused was very bad, but just because two of them are bad it doesn't mean that they all are. The majority of wolves are peace-loving, shy and gentle creatures, no different to you or me. Can we honestly say that it is right to punish the innocent for something we think it's possible they might do in the future? That is the first reason why we should not lock them up.

The second argument for locking them up is that wolves are different to us. If they are different, they are unpredictable. If they are unpredictable, they cannot be trusted. We all like to know how people will behave in situations, so that we can be sure that we are safe. Wolves are not safe, because we don't know how they will act. We can't understand how they communicate with one another, because they use a totally different language. They howl and growl and use body language. We speak English. If we don't understand what they're saying, it is impossible to know what they are thinking and that is dangerous. That is the second reason why we should lock them up.

The second reason we should not lock them up is that it is possible to learn how they communicate. There have been scientists who have studied wolves and have learned what each different howl and growl and body position means. They can explain why wolves act the way they act. If we can learn to understand them, they won't be so scary any more. Perhaps if we learned about them and taught them to understand us as well and showed them that they don't need to be scared of us either, we could all get along better. There is nothing so different or so scary that it can't be made better by a little education and a little understanding. That is the second and most important reason why we should not lock them up.

I have given you the arguments for and against locking wolves up. I know what I think, but it is up to you. What is your opinion?

Roy Alist Lane,
Republicham,
Home Counties,
UK,
RO7 4LZ.

Dear Charlie,

You made an interesting point in your last letter. I know you don't really understand the 'royalist' debate in this country. Things where you live are very different, so I realise it's hard for you to understand. The thing is, as one of the few countries still to be a monarchy, people have often asked whether, in this day and age, it is appropriate to we keep this old-fashioned tradition. There are plenty of arguments for and against. I will try to explain some of them to you.

For about ten years in the seventeenth century, England tried doing without a royal family. We did not do well. The English Civil War usefully showed us that we rather like having a monarch. As soon as Charles II took the throne, after the civil war, the country settled down and we haven't had such a serious attempt to get rid of the royal family since. What this shows is that the English royal family seem to be quite well liked. If they were horrible dictators, we probably would have seen a few more uprisings. As we haven't, we probably don't need to worry too much about kicking them out! This is one very good reason why we should keep the royal family.

On the other hand, some people do get quite cross about the cost of maintaining the royal family. The exact amount is difficult to pin down, but it costs tens of millions of pounds every year to cover the royals' expenses. That money comes from us. When we pay our taxes, some of it goes to the royal family. Wouldn't that money be better off going to the NHS or to our schools? That is one very good reason why we should abolish the royal family.

That said, the royal family does contribute to our economy and our country. Thousands of people visit England every year and many come here because of the royal family. They want to visit Buckingham Palace and they want to see the changing of the guards and they want to experience the culture of royalty. Sometimes being one of the only countries left to have a royal family helps us; it makes this country a bit different to so many others. It gives people a reason to visit us. That is another good reason to keep the royal family.

Equally, keeping our royal family does make England a rather old-fashioned country. The trouble with being old-fashioned is that sometimes things change for a reason. In this country, we no longer have slavery, we now have votes for women and there is no more child labour. Why should we have someone ruling over us? Why should we have a group of people with silly titles to make decisions for us? Why can't we all be equal? At least we get some sort of say over the members of the government – we get to vote. The royals weren't our choice to rule us, so why should they be allowed to? We are all supposed to have equal rights and opportunities. This is clearly not true of the royals. This is another good reason to get rid of the royal family.

As you can see, there are reasons why keeping the royal family is a good idea and reasons why abolishing the royal family is a good idea too. It is hard to make a decision. Honestly, I can't make up my own mind on the subject! What do you think? I look forward to your thoughts.

I'll sign off now, dear Charlie. Do take care of yourself and I hope to hear from you soon.

With love and very best wishes,

Alana x

NEWS

Jack Rose asks: What's better for the gamer - a board or a screen?

In the twenty-first century, there are plenty of opportunities out there to keep yourself entertained. You might be a social media fan. You might be a book lover. You might be a keen sportsman or woman. Or perhaps – just perhaps – you like to play games. Amongst those who like to play games, there tends to be a divide between those who like to play traditional board games and those who like to play computer games. So the question of which is best is a tricky one. I will lay out the arguments for each one and let you decide.

Board gamers would argue that traditional games are the best, because there is no concern about batteries running out or equipment breaking. There are no adverts or updates to install. There is no headache-inducing screen to stare at and the equipment is cheap and cheerful. You can easily stop and get up to fetch a drink or visit the toilet, no matter what stage of play you have reached. All these conveniences are huge advantages to the board gamer. This is one reason that board games are better than computer games.

Computer gamers would argue that there is no need to worry about losing pieces, which mean that you can no longer play effectively. They would argue that you don't need to worry about repeating the questions on flimsy, easy-to-damage cards or knocking over the board and nobody remembering where the pieces were. They might also suggest that being able to add updates keeps the games fresh and exciting, while the opportunity to watch replay videos helps them improve their games. This is one reason that computer games are better than board games.

Nevertheless, board gamers would argue that the majority of board games are fun for families or groups of friends, because they are for people to play together. You can play in teams and have big groups of people all entertained and interacting for ages. This is an advantage over computer games, because the majority of computer games are for one person or, possibly, two. However, there is little or no conversation generated by staring at a screen together, so the social aspect of board games is something that is totally lost when you play computer games. This is another reason that board games are better than computer games.

In comparison to board games, however, computer games tend to generate conversation after the game has been played. There are lots of computer games that have huge followings and are therefore talked about an awful lot, by a huge range of different people. Minecraft, for example, is a game that not only is adored by both young and old, but also has conventions and meetings where its fans can make friends with one another and chat about the game. This is, of course, a great way to meet like-minded people. This is another reason that computer games are better than board games.

As you can see, there are plenty of reasons why board games are great and there are plenty of reasons why computer games are great. This isn't a debate that will be solved by me! Perhaps the solution is simply to have a go at each and not be afraid to switch between the two. They're both great!

- Jack Rose is The Impartial's Features Editor

INSTRUCTION TEXTS

What are instructions?

An instruction text refers to any text that explicitly tells the reader how to do something. This might be as simple as directions to the shops or as complicated as how to put together flat-pack furniture (which, let's face it, is pretty complicated!). It may be a simple list of imperative statements, or it may be a more expanded text. Either way, it will follow what is probably the simplest structure, with the simplest set of features, of any of the text types. That said, don't be fooled into thinking that instruction texts are 'too simple' for children to achieve highly in. Have a look at 'How to Walk the Plank and Live to Tell the Tale' for a really high-quality example of a text with all the features you could ask a high-ability Year Six child to include. However, it is easy for children to underachieve in instruction texts, because of the perception of their simplicity. Therefore, it is important to make your expectations of the children's instruction writing very clear.

Types of text that lend themselves well to instructions: leaflets, speeches, recipes, blogs.

Features of instruction writing[1]

- A short introduction is needed to show why the writer is writing. I would suggest that children do this right from the word go, even in Reception.

- Bullet points are often used, or numbered paragraphs, to organise the writing. This is standard practice and perfectly legitimate, even at upper Key Stage Two.

- Present tense is the most obvious to use for instruction writing, although the more complex text may stray into past tense very occasionally.

- Imperative verbs should be used extensively throughout the text.

- Most instruction texts will be written exclusively in the second person (Tie **your** shoelaces...) although some more complex ones may use the first or third person intermittently (Tie **your** shoelaces tightly when **you're** going for an interview. **I** often find that shoelaces are what let **me** down in stressful situations and interviewers will not be amused if **you** trip and fall in **their** laps.)

- There will often be technical language needed in instruction writing, as the process you are giving instructions for tends to be a technical one (hence the need for instructions).

- Although instruction writing can often be fairly plain and unembellished, one way to up-level writing is to include adverbs, particularly as a sentence opener (**Carefully** unwrap the present, **Quickly** nip downstairs).

- Another way to up-level is through punctuation. Use a colon at the end of the introduction and semi-colons throughout to separate sections.

- Tone should be fairly formal, as a rule, although informality can creep in at the higher levels, in order to achieve a clearer sense of individuality and originality of style.

- Modal verbs will need to be used fairly extensively.

- Similarly to an explanation text, it is useful, though not essential (particularly at Key Stage One), to have a short conclusion.

[1] Naturally, this is an exhaustive list. Class teachers must use their judgement as to which are age-appropriate and ability-appropriate for their children.

How to be good in assembly

We all have to be good in assembly. This is what to do.

- Line up quickly

- Walk to the hall

- Sit down quietly

- Listen and do not talk

- At the end, wait for your teacher to tell you to go

How to Play Tag

Have you ever played Tag? It is a funny game! You can play with your friends and family. Follow these simple rules to learn how to play.

1. First, choose who is going to chase everyone.

2. Next, everybody else must run away.

3. The chaser must stand still and count to ten.

4. After that, the chaser has to try to catch one of the others. He has to say tag when he catches somebody.

5. Next, the person who has been caught is the new chaser.

1 2 3 4 5 6 7 8 9 10

How to make Fairy Dust

Before you begin creating your fairy dust, you should make sure that there are no smelly old trolls around. Trolls are very sneaky and might try to steal your dust to make mischief. If you are wearing any jewellery, you should take it off too. Fairies like sparkly things and they might want to play with your jewellery.

When you have checked for trolls and taken off your jewellery, you should gather these ingredients:

- a small pot of sand

- some colourful glitter

- a jar of food colouring

- at least five beads, pebbles or feathers

As soon as you have these ingredients, you are ready to begin. Follow these steps to create your own magical fairy dust:

- Mix a few drops of food colouring with your pot of sand, so that the sand starts to look bright, like a starry sky.

- Shake some glitter into the pot of sand. You need plenty, because fairies will be attracted to the sparkle. Mix it in.

- When you have finished mixing, check again for trolls. Don't forget that they are very sneaky!

- After that, the sand should look very glittery and colourful. Now it's time to smooth it out. Fairies like very flat surfaces, where they can easily play.

- Finally, you are ready to add the colourful beads, feathers or pebbles. Put these around the edge of your pot of sand. This will give the fairies something to sit on.

Well done. You have made your own fairy dust!

HOW TO BUILD THE PERFECT SNOWMAN

by F Rostee • A Chillz publication

KEEPING BUSY...

When cold weather strikes, it is tempting to huddle indoors and shiver. Therefore, it is easy to miss out on lots of exciting and enjoyable activities. Nobody wants to be stuck inside feeling sad! If you are looking for ideas to spice up your winter, this is the book for you. Read on to find out how to keep yourself warm, toasty and happy this winter.

The best thing to do in snowy weather is build a snowman! Here's how to do it.

You will need:

- A carrot or parsnip
- Some wellies
- A woolly hat
- A pair of gloves
- A woolly scarf
- Some large black stones
- Lots of smaller black stones

METHOD

1. First, find a nice big pile of fresh snow. It is important that you choose snow that is quite new, because otherwise animals might have gone to the toilet in it. Yuck!

2. After that, take a small ball of snow in your hands. Roll this over and over in the big pile of snow until it starts to get bigger and bigger. This will be your head. Set it to one side.

3. When you have finished that, push the rest of the snow into a really big pile and shape it so it looks roughly like a cylinder. This is the body.

4. Next, put the head on top of the body.

5. Use two of the large stones to make eyes and use the rest to make some buttons down the snowman's front. Place the carrot or parsnip underneath the eyes to make a nose.

6. Now you get to do the fun part! Use the smaller stones to make a happy, smiley, friendly mouth.

7. Then, you can get your snowman dressed. Put on his wellies, hat, scarf and gloves.

Your snowman is finished!

MORE IDEAS...

If you enjoyed this snowman leaflet, here are some other leaflets that might interest you:

- How to Make a Volcano
- How to Build the Perfect Model Aeroplane
- Activities that will Definitely Get You Grounded

- Naughty Things to Make and Do
- The Silly Guide to Tickles
- How to Make Your Teacher Cross

HOW TO WALK SAFELY THROUGH THE FOREST

Good evening everyone. Thank you for taking the time to be here tonight. I am here to give you some guidance on walking through the forest safely.

Whenever you walk through the forest, it is important to make sure that you are keeping yourself safe. There are dangers lurking in the trees. Before you set out, be sure to follow these instructions on how to stay out of trouble. You can take notes if you need to, but there will be a handout at the end of this session.

- Unless you are very big and strong, the police advise you to travel through the forest in groups of three or more. Wolves, bears and trolls never attack large groups.

- When visiting elderly relatives in their wooden cottages, set up a password. Before you enter the house, ask them for the password. This will allow you to be sure that an identity thief is not tricking you. Wolves in particular are known to enjoy dressing up.

- Additionally, it is vital that you stay on the main paths. Wandering off the beaten track is a sure way to get yourself lost and getting lost in the forest is very dangerous.

- Avoid picking flowers. They are extremely beautiful, very fragrant and tremendously tempting, I know. However, bending down to pick them leaves you vulnerable. Trolls often wait till you are bending down to push you over and sit on you. Because they are very heavy, this is most unpleasant. Picking flowers could also lead you off the beaten track. As I mentioned before, this is very dangerous.

- Finally, never enter the forest after dark. The forest is terribly scary and treacherous at night. It is difficult to see the beaten track. This makes it especially hard to stay on it. Also, animals have much better night vision than people. This means they can see you, but you can't see them. Not good!

In conclusion, if you follow these simple rules, you will be safe and secure whenever you enter the forest. If you don't, you may get in trouble. Please help yourselves to a printout of these instructions. The printouts are on the table at the back of the room. Thank you for listening and have a safe journey home.

How to bake the yummiest chocolate chip muffins in the world

Caution! Before baking, please bear in mind that these cakes are probably the yummiest cakes there have ever been. They are so delicious, so amazingly delectable, that you will need to be very careful – it has been known for bakers to be mobbed on their way home by people who are simply too overwhelmed by the gorgeous aroma of the finished product. We advise that you keep all doors and windows closed during baking and ensure that you put the finished muffins into smell-proof boxes.

Chocolate chip muffins

Ingredients

250g self-raising flour

25g cocoa powder

175g caster sugar

175ml mild olive oil
(or sunflower oil)

100ml milk

2 medium eggs

1-2 tsp vanilla essence

1 packet chocolate chips

Equipment

12 muffin cases

A 12-hole muffin tin

Timer

Method

1. Carefully and sensibly measure out the ingredients. It is easy to get carried away and excited by the prospect of so much deliciousness. Don't allow yourself to rush! This will spoil the cakes. At this stage, it is also sensible to pop the twelve muffin cases into your muffin tin and turn on your oven (to around 170°C 340°F).

2. Using a wooden spoon, combine all the powdered ingredients (flour, cocoa and sugar) in a large bowl. Stir gently till the ingredients are thoroughly mixed.

3. In a separate, smaller bowl, combine all the wet ingredients (oil, milk, eggs and vanilla essence). Just pour them in together and mix for about twenty seconds – there is no need to beat them.

4. Make a big dent in the centre of the large bowl of powdered ingredients (this is often called a well – it should look like an empty volcano). Pour in the wet ingredients. Mix together, but take care not to over-mix. As soon as the mixture is combined, stop stirring. The more you stir, the more carbon dioxide you remove from the mixture. The more carbon dioxide you remove, the less your muffins will rise when you cook them.

5. Add the chocolate chips and stir once or twice to combine.

6. Dollop the mixture generously into the muffin cases.

7. Carefully slide the muffin tins into the oven and set your timer for 15 minutes. (The muffins will take around 15-20 minutes to cook, so it is sensible to check them after fifteen minutes.) Don't forget to keep all the doors and windows closed during this time. The last thing you want is someone burning themselves trying to eat roasting hot muffins, because they just smell too delicious!

HOW TO WALK THE PLANK – AND LIVE TO TELL THE TALE!

 Good morning all and thank you for joining me. I hope this instructive survival session will be of use to you.

If you are ever captured by pirates (and, let's face it, it could happen at any moment), I'm sure one of your biggest anxieties would be the dreaded plank. Will they make you walk it? Are you a strong enough swimmer to survive until another ship passes by? Will you be attacked by sharks or crocodiles? Well, if you follow these simple instructions, you will no longer have to worry about the plank. It will turn into your dearest ambition – to prove that you are able to escape the pirates' clutches! Read on to find out how...

- First, you must establish yourself as someone not to be trifled with, in order to force the pirates to deal with you. Ensure you are a difficult prisoner in all the little ways you possibly can: shout ill-mannered things at them; bang loudly with your bound feet, so they can't have a conversation; laugh at them when they try to threaten you; and insult their cooking. There is no surer way to get on a pirate's bad side than by being rude about the quality of the catering.

- Once they have decided that you are more trouble than you are worth, they will want to get rid of you as soon as possible. It is customary for pirates to keep prisoners destined for the plank in the crow's nest during the night prior to their fate. This is exactly where you want to be!

- As soon as they shove you into the crow's nest, you must begin your task: using your mouth, work away at the knots tying up your hands. Pirates always use far too much rope and not enough knot to keep their prisoners stuck. This will work to your advantage.

- It will probably take an hour or so to untie the knots. It may feel like longer. Do not panic! This is a standard timeframe and you will still have plenty of time to complete your next task. If there is any rope lying around in the crow's nest, do try to collect it as it will make your next task easier, but don't worry if there isn't. Sometimes pirates are inconsiderate to the would-be escapee prisoner.

- Your next task is to unravel the rope. All rope is made of plaited strands of material. You need to separate out the strands until you are left with several thinner ropes (preferably five or six, but you can get away with four). Set approximately three of these to one side. You will need them in a minute.

- After you have unraveled the rope, tie all the strands together in one long cord (aside from those you set aside earlier). Then tie the end around your waist. You should have plenty left. In the other end, tie a large loop. The loop should be the same size as the floor of the crow's nest. Don't forget to measure it! This is very important. Then hide the loop under your jacket.

- Next, tie your hands back together, using the three strands of rope you set aside earlier. Make sure you do it tightly enough that the pirates won't suspect, but loosely enough that you can slip your hands out quite easily.

- In the morning, all the crew will gather to see you drown. This is your opportunity. When they set you walking the plank, make sure you pretend to be scared. Beg them to save you. If you can possibly manage to cry, this helps; it will make them laugh, so they will be more distracted. As you reach the end of the plank, subtly slip the loop of rope out of your jacket and let it drop to the floor. Carefully and slowly, inch your way to the end of the plank and, using your foot, push the loop onto the plank.

- You are now attached to the plank. When you step off the end, you will end up hanging underneath it. Fortunately, a pirate ship always positions its plank above its kitchen. Remember, all the pirates will be up on deck, watching you 'drown'. This leaves you with the perfect opportunity to scramble through the kitchen window and hide in the larder! Here, you will be safe, warm and have all the food you want. As soon as the pirates reach land, they will all leave the ship to raid the town. This is the time for you to escape!

- There you have it! An absolutely flawless way to walk the plank and live to tell the tale. Thank you for listening and...you're welcome!

RECOUNT TEXTS

What are recounts?

The difficulty with recounts is in keeping them different to narratives. The most usual, accepted definition of a recount is 'to tell a story'. So what makes them different to fictional, narrative writing? The short answer is: nothing. There ought still to be descriptive language, there might still be several characters, there is still a story happening. The difference is that with recounts, there needs to be a degree of formality, which excludes the possibility of extreme poetic license. One would not anticipate e.g. a flashback episode, in a recount. It is a simple description of an event – of something that has happened. It doesn't have to have actually happened (you will note that the biography and autobiography included in this section are those of a sorcerer and a dragonologist, respectively). It has to *be written as though* it has actually happened. That's the crux of the matter. That is where it is different to fiction.

Types of text that lend themselves well to recounts: biographies, autobiographies, newspaper reports, police reports, diaries, letters, emails, postcards.

Features of recount writing[1]

- A recount must always be in the past tense, as the event being described has, obviously, already happened!

- Time conjunctions are vital, in order to sequence events logically.

- As a rule, recounts will be fairly formal in tone. This doesn't mean that there can't be any description, but it should be useful description (e.g. in a police report: 'the suspect had long hair, green eyes and a Metallica t-shirt').

- A recount will always be in either first or third person.

- In order to up-level children's work, grammatical features that can be useful include: prepositional phrases, adverbial phrases and similes. Any language feature that adds clarity to the story is worthwhile.

[1] Naturally, this is an exhaustive list. Class teachers must use their judgement as to which are age-appropriate and ability-appropriate for their children.

My First Day At School

I was four when I started school. It was not what I expected!

I got to school early and met my teacher. His name was Mr. Strong. He was very tall. I was scared of him. Then he smiled at me and he was not scary any more.

Next, Mr. Strong told all the children to sit on the carpet. He read us a good story. It was funny!

Later, it was time for lunch. We went to the hall to eat. I was worried I would get lost, but Mr. Strong showed me the way. Lunch was yummy!

At the end of school, Mr. Strong took me back to my mummy. She asked if I had had a good day. I smiled a lot. My mummy smiled too. It was a very good day.

WHEN I WAS AN EXPLORER!

Good morning children. My name is Eddie the Explorer. I went to Africa last year to see some elephants. Elephants are my favourite animals. There are lots of them in Africa.

First, I went to a special zoo for elephants, but I didn't like it. The elephants were a bit old and dusty. I wanted to see them out in the wild.

After that, I went to a shop and bought a ticket for a safari. A safari is a trip out to the wild to see lots of animals in their natural homes. I was very excited!

Next, I got in a car with a driver called Max. He drove me out into the wild. It took a very long time to get there. Suddenly, I sat up! I could see a lion! There were about seven or eight lions and lionesses. Max told me that a lioness is a female lion. That means it is a girl.

Soon, I began to see big footprints in the dust. They were very very big. I knew they must be elephant footprints! Suddenly, I saw some grey shapes moving around. Elephants! We got so close I could almost touch the elephants. They were beautiful. Some were old, but some were young. They looked like a lovely family.

That is the story of my adventure in Africa.

A Day in the Life of a Cat

My cat is very pretty and sweet, but very lazy. She never wants to play and run. I will tell you about what she did yesterday and you will see how lazy she really is!

First, she was asleep when I woke up in the morning. I went downstairs and she was sleeping in her bed. I knew she would be. She always is! Next, she ate her breakfast. She took ages. Then she went back to bed!

She had a nap for a long time, then got up and went outside to the garden. She played with an orange leaf for a few minutes, but then she went to sit under a chair. She stayed under the chair and watched a butterfly. She didn't bother chasing the butterfly. She was too lazy!

After lunch, I went out to my friend's house. I got back at three o'clock. My cat was asleep on my bed. My dad said she had been under the chair for a while, then she had played with a worm for about ten minutes. Then she had come up to my room and fallen asleep. What a lazy cat!

All that evening, she stayed asleep on my bed. She only moved at bedtime, because I had to get into bed to go to sleep.

You can see, then, that my cat really is very lazy. Mum and Dad say she is a bit more lively at night, but I don't think she is. I think she is the laziest cat in the whole world!

| Name | Kitty L. Uffa | Date of incident | 10th May |
| Time of incident | 3.15pm | Place of incident | Elm Lane |

WHAT HAPPENED?

As I was walking along Elm Lane near my house, I heard footsteps behind me. At first, I didn't look around. I was close to home, so I wasn't really paying attention. Suddenly, I heard a growl. My heart felt like a butterfly, it was beating so fast. I felt a lump of fear in my stomach. Carefully, I peeked over my shoulder. I couldn't see anything. Hoping that my ears were wrong and that I was just being silly, I walked faster and tried to calm down.

Next, things got even scarier. Without warning, something warm, heavy and strong thumped against my back. I couldn't help letting out a loud shriek as I fell to the ground, but the soft, heavy creature rolled off my straight away. As I lay there, I began to shake. It's not every day you get knocked down by some unknown monster, after all.

However, as I slowly raised my head to look at what had pushed me over, I could see that it was no longer interested in me. Its back was towards me and it was padding gently away. I lifted my head and gazed at the magnificent creature. It had black and orange striped fur. It was as big as a pony. It had a long, swishing tail and a proud head, with triangular ears. A tiger! I rubbed my eyes furiously to check I wasn't seeing things. It was still there. A tiger!

The tiger paced majestically away from me, as I lay there in awe, terror and disbelief. I couldn't help but notice how long and strong its claws were, which made me tremble even harder. While I watched, it disappeared round the corner into Chestnut Crescent. As soon as it was out of sight, I scrambled to my feet and made a dash for my house. I bolted inside and locked the doors. That's when I called the police. All the while, I was craning my neck to see out of the window and spot the tiger, but I never saw it again.

| Signature | Kitty L. Uffa | Date | 1st October 2015 |

NEWS

Plenty of 'Space' to Live!

Robert Manson, international businessman and adventurer, shocked the world yesterday when he announced his plans to build up to ten thousand new houses on the moon.

In yesterday's press conference in Munich, Manson explained that he has instructed his architects to design lavish holiday homes for the world's richest people. His plans also include a 384, 800 kilometre escalator to transport his clients to their new houses.

The houses themselves will be extremely luxurious. Features are said to include indoor swimming pools and jacuzzis, four-poster beds in every bedroom, log fires in the living areas and a Michelin-starred chef, trained to cook in zero gravity. A source close to Manson has revealed that the millionaire has been looking into plants that could possibly grow on the moon, in the hopes of creating what he calls 'moon gardens'.

When asked what he estimated the cost to be, Manson laughed and waved his hand airily. "I have no doubt that it will be extremely expensive," he chuckled, "but I have a record of being the first to do things that people think are crazy, reckless or impossibly expensive. There is no way I will let anyone else beat me to this."

Manson's record certainly is impressive. He launched the world's first budget airline, managed a global film and television company and has a personal fortune in the hundreds of millions. Additionally, he has completely several wacky personal challenges, such as travelling around the world in a hang-glider. Will this latest project be doomed to failure or will it be yet another unlikely success story? Only time will tell.

Diary of a Trainee Sorcerer

Dear Diary,

It's been the most incredible day today. I can hardly even compose myself to be able to write about it! My career began today. My career! On this blustery day in November of 1984. The smell of gunpowder and burning wood hung in the air this morning, from the Guy Fawkes celebrations of last weekend. I remember a carpet of leaves, tinted with golden brown, russet red and brilliant orange hues, swirling around my feet as I hurried down the road to college. I love college life (I am studying drama and getting straight As, I have a great group of friends and my parents are really supportive), I was feeling dissatisfied with life in general this morning. I was questioning my passion for the subject I had chosen and I was really questioning where my life was going. Do I want to end up scrabbling around for horrible little jobs playing 'Man with Fungal Infection' in an advert for foot cream? Not really. It's amazing how clearly I remember those moments. Mostly, I remember feeling that I'd reached a crossroad and not knowing which way to turn. Already, it seems a lifetime ago, yet somehow I know it will stay with me forever.

Without a spark of warning, my world froze. That sounds very melodramatic and corny, but it's literally what happened. The cars that had been meandering down the chilly road no longer moved. Exhaust fumes hung static. Droplets of fog stopped their swirling dance. The world seemed to hold its breath. For me, time continued, but for anyone and anything else, it had stopped. My brain ticked rapidly through the options and stopped at the only one that could possibly make sense. Magic. As Sherlock Holmes (one of my favourite literary heroes) might have remarked, 'When you have eliminated the impossible, whatever remains, however improbable, must be the truth'.

Around five of my heartbeats had passed between the freezing of the world and my coming to the conclusion that magic must be involved. I had no way to judge the passage of time other than by my heartbeats, as I wore no watch and the town clock was frozen mid-tick. That's when he appeared. Usually, when people say that someone 'appeared', they mean the person emerged from a doorway or walked out from behind whatever was in front. However, in this instance, I mean he literally appeared out of thin air. Diary, I swear, I have never seen anything like it before. I have never before experienced the incredible feeling that the world had turned upside down and that, no matter what happened next, my life would never be boring again.

I can't remember now the details of our conversation. What stay with me are the emotions he caused within me. You might have expected me to be scared, apprehensive or anxious. Freezing a street and materialising in front of a college student sounds like a perfect way to cause a complete breakdown in that student! To be honest, in those first few moments, I was terrified. However, as soon as he began to talk, I somehow knew that I had nothing to worry about. Oh, Diary, I'm so nervous! I have to pack tonight, as I'm going away with the sorcerer in the morning. I'd better go, but I'll come back and write again when I'm at the scorceror's. That will hopefully be tomorrow! How exciting!

BIOGRAPHY
OF WANDA X. PLORE
DRAGONOLOGIST

Arguably the most famous and influential dragonologist of all time, Wanda X. Plore is credited with discovering no fewer than sixteen new species of dragon. That's more than twice the number discovered by any other dragonologist in the world. However, Wanda appears to have almost stumbled into dragonology by mistake. Certainly, there was no clue from her early life to indicate that she would end up the most famous dragonologist who ever lived.

Wanda was born in a small village in Somerset, the only child of parents Charles (a mechanic at the local garage) and Freda (a housewife). As a child, she attended the local primary school, where she proved an 'unexceptional' student, according to her school reports. From there, she continued on to the local secondary school, which seems to have considered her as unremarkable as she considered it. When I asked her about her education, in an interview conducted in 1996, her answer was short and to the point: 'Dull, uninspiring and extremely forgettable', she laughed, with her trademark twinkle. So how did such an undistinguished beginning turn into such a significant career?

Well, the turning point in Wanda's life appears to have been the year she spent travelling after leaving school with a handful of qualifications and, in her own words, 'a complete lack of skills'. Aged barely seventeen, she and a friend bought tickets to Peru, which was apparently 'the cheapest ticket we could find'! They had been trekking in the mountains of Peru for just three days when Wanda encountered her first dragon. That was the moment that her life took off. Rather than running, screaming in terror, from the fire-breathing monster in front of her (as, by all accounts, her somewhat more timid friend immediately did), Wanda stood utterly still, fascinated by the bizarre and wonderful creature before her. Through pure chance, the species she had encountered was one of only two in the entire world which cannot breathe fire. Luck was on Wanda's side that day...and she made the most of it.

Within that first year, Wanda's travel plans became, as she says herself, 'all about the dragons'! She met several more species, although she became much more cautious about how she approached them, buying the appropriate fire-resistant clothing and portable fire-extinguisher, just in case. By the time she returned home, her detailed and extensive notes were already attracting attention. She had sent them to her mother, Freda, for safekeeping and it seems that luck was once again on her side, for Freda, unbeknownst to her daughter, had once dated the celebrated Danish dragonologist (then living in London) Singe D'Eyebrows. Perhaps recognising her daughter's early talent, or maybe just in an attempt to promote her daughter's work, Freda showed Wanda's notes to Singe, who at once became, according to Freda's account to her daughter, 'almost incoherent with delight'. Did Singe realise that he had discovered the greatest dragonologist of all time? Perhaps not. But he knew that he was on to something!

Back in England, Wanda travelled to London to meet Singe and there began one of the most important and exciting working relationships in the history of dragonology. Singe taught her everything he knew, Wanda taught him everything she had so recently discovered and the rest, as they say, is history. Who could have guessed that from such humble beginnings would grow such an incredible scientist? Wanda's story truly is a lesson for us all; demonstrating the rewards of perseverance, enthusiasm and, not least, experimentation.

REPORT TEXTS

What is a report?

A report is defined in the dictionary as 'to give a spoken or written account of something that one has observed, heard, done or investigated'. At first glance, this seems extremely close to the definition of a recount. However, the major difference between a recount and a report is that a recount is, essentially, a story of something that has happened. A report is a piece of information writing about EITHER an event, a place, a person, an object, a scientific experiment – really about anything. What this means is that it doesn't need to be in time order and there will often be additional information, which is not directly involved in the 'story' of what has taken place. For example, in a report of a science experiment, you would probably include a list of equipment. In a recount of a science experiment, you would not do this; the equipment might be referred to, but only as and when it was used within the 'story'.

Historically, newspaper reports have often been re-categorised as recounts. This makes sense, from one point of view, as they often tell a story of an event, in order, and sometimes don't include any additional information outside of the story. This lends itself well to a recount. However, similarly to argument texts, we need to be clear that a newspaper report is **called** a report for a reason. Yes, some will be reporting on events, simply retelling the story in order, and therefore be closer to recounts than the strict definition of a report. However, if we are going to teach children skills that they are going to translate to the real world, why are we confusing the issue by telling them that a newspaper **report** is actually a recount? As the name would suggest, this is not only inaccurate, but very confusing. The easiest way to tackle this confusion is to explain that there are different types of newspaper **article**. Some are recounts of events. Some are reports. Some are editorials. It is important to be clear on the difference and try not to use confusing terminology.

Types of text that lend themselves well to reports: newspaper reports (!), information leaflets, guide books, encyclopaedia entries, magazine articles, text books, letters, blogs, emails.

Features of report writing[1]

- A report should always be written in the third person.

- It needs an introduction and a conclusion, but the middle section is not necessarily chronological. It might be! But it equally might not be.

- There is likely to be a substantial amount of writing in the passive voice. Some active may be used, but it will be overwhelmingly passive.

- There will be a move from generalised information to more specific detail as the report moves on (Some drugs have been recovered from the scene of the crime. Police revealed that fifty kilos of heroin were found, in addition to several 'legal highs' such as those known as 'Clockwork Orange').

- Structural features such as bullet points are acceptable in a report.

- Grammatical features such as rhetorical questions, patterns of three and adverbials may be used.

- A report's conclusion should summarise the findings or the information and may either give recommendations for the future or elicit inferences from what has happened.

[1] Naturally, this is an exhaustive list. Class teachers must use their judgement as to which are age-appropriate and ability-appropriate for their children.

The Playground Party

All of the children in this school held a party in the playground yesterday. There were two hundred children there and there were twenty adults too.

The children played games and the adults stood around chatting. The games the children played were lots of fun. They played Tag, Stuck-in-the-Mud, football and held races for each class.

The PTA was selling cakes and drinks. They were delicious cakes. Some were chocolate and some were lemon. There were hot drinks for the adults and squash or water for the children.

Many of the children wore fancy dress. The theme was fantasy characters, so there were plenty of fairies, witches and superheroes.

Everyone had a wonderful time. The party was a great success. The PTA hopes to run it again next year.

NEWS

Sleepy Sunday SHOCK

On Sunday morning, the villagers of Sleepton were shocked to find a whole castle full of people living in the wood.

The wood had been very overgrown and dark for a hundred years, so nobody from Sheepton ever went in. Everyone thought that only animals lived there.

Everyone was very surprised on Sunday when the wood suddenly vanished! Lots of people were too scared to go near the castle. They thought that the castle must be magical and they were worried that the wood might grow back suddenly and trap them.

In the afternoon, a group of nice soldiers came down to the village. They were from the castle. They told everyone not to be afraid of the castle. They explained that a spell had made everyone in the castle fall asleep for a hundred years, but now the spell was broken. The villagers were very pleased.

Now, the villagers and the people from the castle are beginning to make friends.

NEWS

JIMMY AND THE SWING

Seven-year-old James Masterson, from Hollow End in Dunstable, set a world record last week for the longest swing ever!

Little Jimmy's record-breaking swing lasted for thirteen hours and sixteen minutes, until he was forced to stop to go to the toilet. The previous record was held by John Baker, from Galloway in Scotland. John managed to swing for ten hours and seven minutes. After that he stopped, because he started to feel a bit sick.

Ellen Masterson, Jimmy's mum, was there to cheer him on. Donald Masterson, Jimmy's dad, stayed at home to look after Jimmy's three younger sisters. Their names are Anna, Susie and Jane. All the family members are very proud of Jimmy's swinging.

Next, Jimmy hopes to enter the Olympic swinging competition. He is continuing to

N E W S

PARTY AT THE PALACE

Starlight City was bustling with visitors yesterday, all celebrating the royal wedding of Prince Bestia and his new bride, Princess Belle.

The celebrations were particularly joyous on this occasion, because the city had been forced to wait a long time for the wedding. Although Prince Bestia was always very handsome and clever, he was famous for his unkind tongue and selfish heart. Servants and visitors to the castle were often sent away either crying or furiously angry. However, at the age of eighteen, Prince Bestia stopped coming out of the castle, closed all the doors and windows and wasn't seen for several years. There were even rumours that he had died. Therefore, Starlight City was overjoyed last year to discover that he was not only alive, but also engaged!

Yesterday's wedding saw the happy prince wed his beautiful and beloved fiancée, Princess Belle. Belle was relatively unknown before the engagement. She is not rich and has no family connections. However, the people of Starlight City don't care at all, because she is the one who has made their prince happy and kind. For that, as well as her kind and gentle spirit, they adore her.

"She's a dear girl," said M. Cog-Zworth, the palace butler. "She has made the prince so happy, I hardly recognise him. It's wonderful."

"We all love her," was the opinion of Lumi Air, the first footman. "She turned the prince back into a man! A better man, I mean, of course. She turned him into a better man. He is very lucky and so are we."

Whenever the prince and princess have been seen in public since their engagement last year, it has been obvious to everyone how deeply they care for one another. Now that they are married, a spokesperson from the palace has announced that they will be away for two weeks on their honeymoon. After they return, they will be settling in Starlight Palace permanently. Who knows? Perhaps there will be another Starlight City celebration next year. Indeed, perhaps the city won't even have to wait a year. Nine months might be enough!

666 Fiery Furnace Folly,
Beaston,
DR4 6ON

8th January 2014

Dear Mr Scale-Fang,

I am writing to you to give you some information on a brand new form of dragon that I have discovered. I think that it should be put into your 'Encyclopedia of Dragons' so that everyone can find out about it.

Its name is the Volcano Dragon. Interestingly, it is in the same family as the Lava Dragon and the dragons that live on Molten Rock.

The Volcano Dragon looks the same as most dragons. It has black wings, a scaly back and a long tail. It is a raging red colour and its teeth look like lumps of fiery coal. The main distinguishing feature of the Volcano Dragon is that it has five black spots on each leg, each of which can open up and release a poisonous gas into the air when it feels threatened.

The Volcano Dragon lives on Mount Etna, in Italy. They like to eat a special root called tapast, which only grows on Mount Etna. Scientists believe that the root is what gives them their raging red colour.

The most interesting fact about the Volcano Dragon is that it is the only animal that has ever been known to learn sign language. Many of them can use up to 200 signs! It has been suggested that the dragons could even be used to carry secret messages for spies. However, this has not yet been tested.

I look forward to hearing from you.

Yours sincerely,

Mr Maytham

Mr Maytham

NEWS

TEENAGE TERROR TERRIFIES TODDLER

A toddler was terrified last night, after a teenage hooligan broke into his parents' house in Bear Wood, stole his dinner and broke his chair. Police are still searching for the girl, who is described as having long, curly, blonde hair; green eyes, with flecks of hazel in them; and a blue dress with white polka dots.

The child's parents, Mr and Mrs Bear, are very angry with the young thief. "We are furious!" said Mr Bear, this morning. "Poor Baby Bear couldn't sleep at all last night, because he was so upset. After we saw the broken chair and the empty, abandoned bowl that was overturned on the table top, we thought perhaps they had been blown by the wind. However, when we saw that somebody was asleep in our poor little son's bed, we realised that she was the one to blame. I blame myself for allowing her to escape before the police arrived, but I will not rest until she is brought to justice! She mustn't get away with this!"

Sadly, it seems that attacks like these are becoming more and more frequent. Only last week, on the other side of Bear Wood, Mrs. Grandma Hood's house was broken into and her clothes were stolen. In comparison to the case of little Baby Bear, Grandma Hood was lucky, as the thief, whose name was Mr. Wolfe, was quickly caught by the local woodcutter, who happened to be passing at the time of the attack. Despite this, several local residents have described the mood in the area as 'uneasy'.

Unfortunately, the police have so far had no luck tracking down the young lady responsible for this latest crime. All residents of Bear Wood and the local area are being asked to look out for anyone who matches the description of the hooligan. Meanwhile, if you have any information, please contact Detective Ginger-Breadman at Can't Catchme Police Station. Officers have warned that the suspect is thought to be armed and dangerous – she was spotted early this morning by a group of dwarfs with a basket of what experts have described as "probably poisoned" apples – and should not be approached on any account.

3 Goat Lane,
Under Bridgeton,
Essex,
BG1 1CC

Dear Sir,

Many thanks for your letter of the 4th April. You are correct that I am the foremost expert in the biology of the common troll and I thank you for your kind words regarding my latest book: 'How to Avoid Troll-Pox'. It sounds to me that the troll behaviour and features you describe are most likely to be those of the Mountain Troll. Therefore, I have included some information on this most fearsome of beasts below. I hope it is of use to you.

Of the many different breeds of troll, there is none more formidable and deadly than the terrible Mountain Troll. Other types may have more publicity – the Mountain Troll's close relative, the Bridge Troll, for example, has been popularized by the famous explorer Billy Goat-Scruff – but the Mountain Troll is by far the largest, fiercest and most aggressive. It is important to know this creature's features and habits if you are planning to visit any of its known locations, as it is easy to identify and avoid if you take a few simple precautions.

First and foremost among the Mountain Troll's identifying features is its size. It is, quite simply, enormous. Indeed, the largest Mountain Troll ever recorded weighed the same as a Ford Focus! Naturally, this is by no means their standard size, but an average adult will be approximately the same size and weight as a small horse. While their large size can seem intimidating and does place them at quite an advantage in comparison to the average human, it does have its benefits. For example, they are, obviously, very easy to spot from a distance. This means that a watchful explorer has nothing to fear from this species.

Another thing that it is important to remember about the Mountain Troll is its habitat. It is all too easy to look at the Mountain Troll's name and dismiss it as an exclusively mountain-dwelling creature. Nothing could be further from the truth. In fact, the Mountain Troll was so named because it is formed primarily from igneous rock. Its hairy appearance is actually due to the moss that grows on its craggy body. Ninety percent of recorded Mountain Trolls actually live in the forests of South America. The other ten percent are dotted around the woods of central Europe. So next time you are booking a holiday to a nice wooded area, remember to ask whether there are any local Mountain Trolls!

The final important thing to know, if you are trying to avoid being eaten by a Mountain Troll, is that Mountain Trolls are nocturnal. It is very rare to see a Mountain Troll abroad in daylight. Occasionally, young Mountain Trolls will stir during the day (much as human babies will wake at night) and occasional sightings have been recorded. It is imperative that you do not approach one of these babies. If a young troll is wandering alone, you can be sure that its mother is looking for it and you do not want to be found near a troll baby by a grumpy troll mother – she will eat you before you have time to blink. Keep your distance! That being said, this situation is very unlikely. You are much more likely to meet a troll at night, so the hours of darkness are when you should be particularly wary.

In conclusion, while the Mountain Troll is an extremely dangerous creature, it is very easy to spot and avoid if you know what you are doing. Avoid wooded areas at night and you will be safe! My advice to you, therefore, is to continue to allow your daughter to visit her grandmother (she is a dear little thing; I particularly liked her little red cloak in the photograph you enclosed). Just ensure that she leaves her grandmother's cottage well before dark, to ensure that she is not in the forest after nightfall.

Yours most faithfully,

Mr. T. Hunter

Mr. T. Hunter

EXPLANATION TEXTS

What is an Explanation?

An explanation is best defined as 'a way of making things clear'. You explain something in order to help your reader understand it better. This means giving factual information on the topic your reader wants to find out about, clarifying any possible misunderstandings and showing either why it is the case or how it is known. It might be helpful to break a piece of writing down, particularly in reception and Key Stage One, and provide the children with section headings. Ideally, these section headings should be created with the children's input. At Key Stage One, this will encourage children to stick closely to explaining, rather than going off on a tangent and ending up persuading or narrating. It will also help them with structuring their writing and including the correct elements. At Key Stage Two, this will encourage children to write in paragraphs and give them an idea of structure (although by the end of Key Stage Two, they should be able to create their own paragraph headings).

Explanation texts are generally chronological, where appropriate (see How Flowers Grow). If it can be done in time order, with time conjunctions, it should be.

Types of text which lend themselves well to an explanation include: letters, textbooks, information leaflets, encyclopaedia entries (online or paper).

Features of an explanation text[1]

- At Key Stage One, explanation texts do not require much in the way of an introduction. The section headings are enough to direct the reader as to the expected content. At Key Stage Two, a short introduction is required, but could be based on the section headings.

- An explanation should always be primarily written in the present tense, with some past tense at the higher levels, to give context. It would be unusual to use the future tense for an explanation

- It is usual to find some technical vocabulary in an explanation; scientific, historical, geographical (etc.) terminology may be necessary.

- Modal verbs are usually necessary for an explanation.

- Rhetorical questions are a great way to introduce an explanation and can be used as section headings.

- Imperatives such as 'Read on to find out' work well at the end of the introduction.

- The imperative sentences could be followed by an ellipsis, as a way of linking the introduction to the rest of the content.

- Paragraphs/sections should be clearly focused on one idea, giving facts, evidence and information about that idea. Generally, the structure of the paragraph is: introduce topic, give information about that topic, give reasons why this information is the case (see the Tooth Gnome paragraph in How Tooth Fairies Collect Teeth).

- Linking conjunctions, particularly those of time and/or cause, should be used in and between paragraphs. Useful ones include: similarly, as well as, additionally, because of this, therefore, furthermore, equally, also, next, then.

- The passive voice will quite often be used in explanation texts, to retain a degree of formality.

- Useful phrases include: 'the reason for this is', 'this means that', 'in fact', 'this is why'.

- At Key Stage One, a conclusion is not necessary. Similarly to the introduction, the section headings are enough. At Key Stage Two, children should begin to include a short conclusion (see How Tooth Fairies Collect Teeth).

[1] Naturally, this is an exhaustive list. Class teachers must use their judgement as to which are age-appropriate and ability-appropriate for their children.

How does a flower grow?

Most flowers grow from seeds. First, the seed needs to be put into soil. This is so that it can eat and drink. The soil has food and water to feed the little seed. It starts to grow roots first. It is important that the roots come first. The roots keep the plant steady, so it doesn't fall over.

Next, the seed needs to be watered. There is not enough water in the soil to keep the seed happy. That is why we need to add extra water to the soil to let the seed drink.

Then the plant begins to grow up. It grows a little white shoot first. This pokes up above the soil and looks for the sun. The plant needs energy from the sun to make it grow. This helps it grow its leaves. The leaves take more energy from the sun. The roots keep eating the food in the soil and drinking the water.

In the end, a little bud grows on the top of the plant. It opens up its petals on a sunny day, so it can see the sun and take energy from it. It is pretty, so bees and butterflies come to visit it. They drink the sweet nectar from inside the flower. They rub their legs against the flower and get pollen on their legs. Then they fly to another plant and mix the pollen into the new plant. The plants use the pollen to make new seeds. The seeds fall to the ground and everything starts again.

SUPERHEROES

WHAT IS A SUPERHERO?

Superheroes are ordinary people, just like you and me. The only thing that is different is their power. All superheroes have a special power. Some have more than one power. Their power is normally linked to their senses. A superhero might have very good hearing or be able to see through walls. Some can smell really well. That would not be nice in public toilets!

WHAT DO SUPERHEROES DO?

Superheroes use their special powers to help people. They are kind and caring, so they always try to rescue anyone who is in trouble. Then they take the bad guys to prison. This is a full time job. On Saturdays and Sundays, they do not get time off! This is why we should all be grateful to superheroes.

HOW DO PEOPLE BECOME SUPERHEROES?

There are lots of different ways of becoming a superhero. Unfortunately, none of them are very nice. Some superheroes are bitten by animals. These animals are usually spiders or cats, which have been changed by scientists. Being bitten does not sound very nice! Other superheroes are aliens, who have been left behind on Earth. Being left on a different planet by your family does not sound very nice either! If you are not a superhero already, it is probably not a very good idea to try to become one. The powers may be nice, but it sounds like becoming one is not very nice!

HOW DO COOKERS WORK?

HOW DINNERS GET HOT

When you eat your dinner in the evening, do you ever wonder how it got so hot? You probably already know that it's hot because it's been in the oven, but have you ever wondered how ovens actually work? Read on to find out!

SWITCHING ON THE OVEN

When grown ups turn on the oven, they usually twist a dial. This dial has numbers on. The higher the number you choose to turn the dial to, the hotter the oven will get. This is because there are hundreds of teeny tiny dragons living in the back of your oven. As grown ups turn the dial, teeny tiny doors open at the back of the oven. If they turn the dial to 200, 200 teeny tiny doors open to reveal 200 teeny tiny dragons. The dragons wake up as soon as their doors open and begin to breathe fire.

COOKING FOOD

It takes a little while for the dragons' teeny tiny flames to make the oven hot enough to cook food, so there is usually a little light on the outside of the oven which flicks off when the dragons have made enough fire. This light is operated by a miniature troll. The reason trolls are used to operate these lights is that trolls don't need thermometers to measure temperature. They are able to judge how hot it is using a special sensor on the top of their heads. As soon as the troll decides it is hot enough, he or she will flick the light off. That's how grown ups know that it is time to put the food in to cook.

Now you know how ovens work! It's a lot more interesting than you thought, isn't it?

HOW ANTS EAT DINNER

Good afternoon. Thank you for coming. I am here today to talk to you about ants. You have probably seen lots of different types of ants scuttling around all over the place. However, have you ever considered how these ants behave when you are not around? Have you thought about where they live or what they eat? Keep listening to find out a bit more about them.

Ants come in all different shapes and sizes. The smallest ant species is called carebara atoma. They are around one millimetre long! The largest ant species is called the African Driver. The biggest of these can be over five centimetres long! Some ants are carnivorous. This means they eat only meat, although this doesn't mean the type of meat that you and I eat. It means insects, worms and spiders. Some ants are herbivorous. This means they eat only plants. Most ants are omnivorous. This means that they eat meat and plants, just like most people.

However, the most interesting thing about ants is the way they actually eat their food. When they have gathered enough for the whole colony, every ant has a special sensor that vibrates on the underside of their stomach. This is the signal to meet in the colony's dining hall for a meal. On the way to the dining hall, the ants each make sure that they have the essential ingredient they all need for a meal. That essential ingredient is a top hat. No ant would dare to turn up to dinner without his or her top hat. The queen would throw them out of the colony and they wouldn't get any food at all. Most ant top hats are made out of hollowed out twigs or acorns, but there are often a few fancy-pants ants wearing sparkly top hats woven from crystals of sugar.

Whenever ants are sharing a meal, they sit at long tables made of leaves. These tables are very handy. Leaves don't stay fresh and suitable for use as a table for very long, so they can only be used for one meal. Any mess that is made during the meal is just swept into the middle of the leaf. The leaf can then be bundled up and taken outside. This is a nice, easy way to keep the anthill tidy and clean.

There you are. Now you know! Ants really are much more interesting than you thought. Thank you for listening. I will now take any questions you might have.

HOW DO TREES GROW IN BRICKLAND?

Most of us know what is needed to make plants and trees grow. They need water, nutrients from the soil and sunlight. However, have you ever wondered how they actually grow? What makes them get bigger? Read on to find out.

SEEDS AND BULBS

Inside every acorn, seed or bulb, there is an unbelievably tiny army of builders. If the seed is really small and will only create a small flower, like a tulip or a pansy, there will be around one hundred builders. If the seed is a little bigger, there could be up to five hundred. Once the seed becomes larger again and needs to be made into a tree, there will be several thousand builders.

MIXING AND BUILDING

As soon as the builders receive the materials they need to build the plant, they begin to work. First, the mixer builders mix the water and soil together to make a paste. Next, they heat it in tiny microwaves, using the sunlight. This makes the paste into bricks, which the construction builders can then use to build the new part of the plant. Meanwhile, the demolition builders push and smash a little hole in the side of the seed, for the root to escape from. As soon as the hole is ready and the bricks have been microwaved, the construction builders get to work to make the root. They work from the inside out, which is why roots and shoots are always thin when they first start to grow, but quickly get thicker.

ROOTS AND SHOOTS

Have you ever wondered why the roots of every plant always start to grow first? There is a simple reason for this. The mixer builders need as much soil as they can get to make the bricks for the construction builders. If the construction builders burrow down into the soil first, they will be able to provide the mixer builders with as much soil as they need to make the millions of tiny bricks they will use in creating the plant.

There you have it. You will no longer have to wonder how plants get bigger, because now you know!

WHAT HAPPENS IN SCHOOLS DURING THE SCHOOL HOLIDAYS?

Good morning everyone. Thank you for coming. I am here today to give you some top secret information and I'm afraid I will have to ask that everyone signs the copy of the Official Secrets Act that is situated on the table at the rear of the hall. You can do that on the way out. As you know, I am here today to explain what happens in schools in the summer holidays. There is something forlorn about an empty school building. When you look at it, you can almost hear the echoes of children laughing, teachers scolding and pens scribbling. I know that many of you have imagined that it is quiet, dusty and abandoned. Nothing could be further from the truth. Let me explain.

The first week of the summer holidays is lovely for a lot of children. The whole summer stretches ahead, full of fun and exciting plans. There is a lot of anticipation in that first week, because, truly, anything could happen. As much as we all love seeing our friends and learning new and interesting things in school, it is nice to have some time to play and have a bit more free time. This is why it feels so wonderful to have a summer holiday – to have more control over what you are doing during the day.

Unfortunately, this feeling isn't shared by everyone. The school building may look abandoned from the outside, but that is only because children make up around ninety percent of people in the school at any one time. The school building is not entirely abandoned, because it still contains ten percent of its population. The teachers. As the day begins, gradually, the teachers emerge. Some crawl, yawning, out of stationery cupboards, pulling pens and paperclips out of their hair. These are the ones who didn't even make it home, because they were missing their classes so much that they slept in the cupboard full of the exercise books full of the children's work. Some arrive in their cars, eagerly scanning the playground for their pupils before feeling their hearts sink when they remember it's the holidays. This is because teachers have very

poor start-up mechanisms. Before their morning cup of coffee in the staffroom, their memories don't kick in, so it is impossible for them to recall the day of the week, let alone the date of the month.

What do they do all day? Plan lessons. Pretending they are simply trying to get a head start on the year ahead, they sadly fill pages and pages of paper with their enthusiastic ideas for fun activities to do with the children they are missing so badly. This is the teachers' way of filling the empty hours until their pupils return. On occasion, when they are feeling particularly anxious, they roam the hallways, desperately searching for someone – anyone – to teach something to. This is because teaching is less of a career and more of a sickness. When you are a teacher, it is impossible to go for too long without imparting wisdom to someone. It has even been known for teachers to stop people in the streets and begin reciting the names of the wives of Henry VIII if their summer holidays go on for too long.

Finally, the sun begins to go down and the discontented teachers return to their beds (whether this is an actual bed or a pile of exercise books). They need to sleep, because in dreams they are transported back to the classroom. This is the only thing that keeps most teachers going, during the summer holidays. Indeed, there is currently a government research project that is experimenting with placing teachers into an induced coma every summer. The difficulty teachers have had with this way of getting through the psychological torment of the holidays is that there isn't enough time to get all their work done. Next time you pass a school building in the summer holidays, spare a thought for the sad and lonely residents. The building may seem abandoned, but it's really not.

Thank you for listening. Please remember to sign the Official Secrets Act at the back of the room as you leave and have a safe journey home.

HOW DO TOOTH FAIRIES COLLECT TEETH?

You may have wondered how the Tooth Fairy manages to remove children's lost teeth from their rooms at night. You may have wondered how it is possible for her not to wake the children and where all her money comes from. If so, read on to discover how it all works.

The Tooth Gnome

The first thing you need to know about the Tooth Fairy is that the name is a little bit misleading. In fact, there are several Tooth Fairies who all work together to collect teeth on behalf of the Tooth Gnome. He is a pleasant, elderly chap who lives in a large burrow underneath Mount Everest. Gnomes, by nature, are rather hairy and the Tooth Gnome is the hairiest of the lot. In fact, he's so hairy that he rather resembles a very large bear, except, of course, that he walks upright. The locals have their own name for him, which you may already know. When the Tooth Fairies have collected the teeth, they send them off to the Tooth Gnome for safekeeping. The reason the teeth have to be looked after is that if nasty goblins or witches got hold of them, they would be able to cast spells on the children who lost them. This is why the Tooth Gnome goes to such lengths to take care of them – he is a very kind and generous gnome.

Division of labour

Each Tooth Fairy has his or her own route; rather like a paper round. You may think that all Tooth Fairies are girls, but nothing could be further from the truth! Tooth Fairies can be girls or boys, just like humans. They each have a small area to look after. It has to be a small area, because otherwise they would not be able to monitor all the children closely enough to know when their teeth are loose. In the past, Tooth Fairies used to use animals to help them. The animals would pass on information about children's loose teeth, so that the Tooth Fairies could keep their records updated. Have you ever seen a dog barking at the sky for no reason? Perhaps you have heard a cat yowling at a tree. Either way, you were probably witnessing communication between a Tooth Fairy and his or her network of animal agents. However, that is quite an old fashioned way of doing things. These days, most Tooth Fairies just use CCTV.

Magic

How does the Tooth Fairy get in and out of a child's bedroom at night without waking the child? That's a good question. Well, Tooth Fairies, like other magical creatures, have access to a variety of products to help them keep out of sight of humans. All the fairies have to do is pop down to their local M&S (Magic and Spells) supermarket and pick up some Sleep Dust. The Tooth Gnome is very generous with expense claims, so it doesn't cost them a penny. Gently and carefully, they blow the dust into the child's nostrils. After that, they can make as much noise as they want, which is lucky, because they have quite a lot to do once they get to the pillow stage.

Tooth removal

Once they are sure that the child is asleep, the Tooth Fairy gently removes the tooth from under the pillow (or wherever the child has placed it). He or she gets out their measuring instruments and check the size, density and clarity – a bit like the way a jeweller would check a precious gem. The reason they have to do this is because several children have, in the past, tried to get away with passing off animal teeth as their own. These greedy children have made it necessary for the Tooth Fairies to be very careful to be sure of the quality of the products they pay for. Their instruments are very delicate and precise; they are made of spiders' webs, leaf skeletons and beeswax (all 100% organic, naturally). As soon as they are sure that the tooth is genuine, they remove a small amount of money from a sealed container (woven from grass) and place it under the child's pillow. The tooth can then be put into the container and it can be re-sealed and sent to the Tooth Gnome (via snail mail).

Paperwork

Lastly and inevitably, the Tooth Fairies have paperwork to complete. The tooth's measurements must be kept on file, the amount of money left has to be recorded and their time must be accounted for. Last year, the Tooth Gnome asked the Tooth Fairies to complete a time and motion study, in order to ascertain the breakdown of how efficiently the teeth were being collected. However, this was withdrawn almost immediately when he learned that 53% of the Tooth Fairies' time was being spent filling out the time and motion study. Nowadays, the paperwork is much swifter and more efficient. This concludes the tooth-gathering process.

There you are – now you know! There is a lot more to the Tooth Fairy than meets the eye. Magic, measurements and dental monitoring: that's what the job of a Tooth Fairy is about.

HOW TO USE CHUNKING GRIDS

A chunking grid is a fantastic tool for children to use both to analyse what they are reading and to plan their own writing. In the pages to come, you will find blank, differentiated chunking grids, appropriate for Key Stages One and Two. You will also find partially completed chunking grids for each year group. The best way to explain how to use them is, as always, by modelling:

Model text:

Trembling, Alana called into the darkness, "Hello? Is there anybody there?" With nervous fingers, she fumbled breathlessly for the light switch, but encountered only blank, unhelpful wallpaper. Suddenly, a rustle. A rat? A fox? Or something more sinister still? Pushing such thoughts firmly aside, Alana swallowed the fear that filled her throat and tried again, 'Excuse me? Please? I need your help."

STRUCTURE	CONTENT	EFFECT		LANGUAGE AND PUNCTUATION
First sentence	Starts with someone speaking: dialogue	We wonder who Alana is and who she's talking to: we feel curious	Help us understand that she is feeling nervous Help set the mood: we feel anxious about her	Descriptive verb: trembling Questions: "Hello? Is there anybody there?"
Through first paragraph	Describes where she is: a room/shed? There is a noise: a rustle	Makes us wonder why she is there What makes a 'rustle'? An animal? Someone hiding?	Describes what the place is like and how she is feeling Makes reader feel nervous	Adjectives and adverbs: nervous, breathlessly, blank, unhelpful
End of first paragraph	She asks for help	We wonder why she needs help We feel sorry for her	Make us feel anxious We know she is scared and feel sorry for her	Question marks in dialogue Uses the word 'fear'

STRUCTURE	CONTENT	EFFECT	LANGUAGE AND PUNCTUATION
First sentence	Opens with character asking a question in unknown, spooky location	Sets up curiosity in reader – why is she scared? Who else is there? We become anxious about the character. / Immediate mood created; Hint at spooky setting; Straight into character's point of view; Set up unknown factors and create anxiety; All this creates a tense, anxious mood	Fronted adverbial: "Trembling"; Prepositional phrase: "into the darkness"; Inverted commas: dialogue; Repeated question marks
Through first paragraph	Description of setting; Description of character's mood; Description of unexpected noise	Creates curiosity; where is the character? Creates empathy with character and thereby tension; Creates tension due to curiosity / More insight into mood; Makes even setting seem 'out to get' her; Heighten pace/tension; Create anxiety and curiosity; Increase anxiety and curiosity, because they're vague and unsettling	Fronted adverbial: "With nervous fingers"; Personification: "unhelpful"; Short sentences: "A rat?" "A fox?"; Rhetorical questions: "A rat? A fox?"; Non-specific description
End of first paragraph	Description of character's mood; Character asks questions again and asks for help	Creates empathy with character; Sets up sympathy for character and makes reader feel curious / Gives insight into character's feelings; Creates empathy; Shows us character's point of view and sets up still more unknown quantities; Increases pace and gives jerky, anxious rhythm; Changes our ideas about to whom character may be speaking	Fronted adverbial: "Pushing such thoughts firmly aside"; Metaphor "fear that filled her throat"; Questions in dialogue "Excuse me? Please?"; Short sentence: "I need your help"; Personal pronoun

From the two (KS2) examples, you can see how chunking grids can be used at different levels, depending on the age and ability of the children. At Key Stage One, we suggest that you remove the 'effect' column, as children can find this challenging. Your higher ability Year 2s may be able to create their own grids, based on those in this book. However, the expectation is that these grids are a teaching tool for you, as the teacher, which you can verbally complete with the children on the board or flipchart. This will allow them to see the breakdown of how writers have created their texts, without putting too much pressure on them. However, even at Key Stage One, when you remove the 'effect' column, they should still be encouraged to discuss effect verbally – children are often surprisingly aware of writers' intentions and they should always be aware that writers have a purpose when they choose vocabulary.

The most effective teaching sequence for Key Stage Two, when you are planning to use chunking grids, would be to encourage the children to highlight language features (we call this 'technique spotting') which they find effective, using the appropriate terminology to label them. Then as a class, in guided groups or (once they are more familiar and confident with the technique) in small, unguided groups, discuss what the effect actually is, how it is achieved and consider either a) how it could be reproduced using different vocabulary or b) how the effect could be altered using different vocabulary. The children should then use a very similar table to plan their own writing, to a set of criteria given by (or, preferably, generated with) the teacher. They should be looking to use either the same or very similar grammatical structures and always considering the effect they are trying to create.

In order to achieve appropriate differentiation, the main factor to consider is teacher talk. It is easy and really helpful, particularly upon introducing chunking initially, to highlight the main features you expect the children to find in order for them to have something to refer to when they are technique spotting. This can be done in written form, but should always be communicated verbally as well. The more complex aspect of differentiation comes from the discussion of effect and modelling the completion of the effect column. As I mentioned earlier, even in the Key Stage One grid, where there is no effect column, there should still be a focus on effect in the teacher talk. This is crucial and must be appropriate to the ability of the children you are working with. Asking high quality questions regarding the specific effects being created by individual words, phrases and grammatical constructions will allow children the opportunity to delve deeply into their reading and fully appreciate the thought that has gone into it.

Some useful questions might be:

- What would be the effect of removing/changing that word?

- Why has the writer repeated that word/phrase/structure?

- Which part of the sentence makes us feel like that?

- What sort of language feature is this?

- Which do you think is the most effective sentence? Why?

- What if the paragraph stopped here? How would that change the effect?

- Can you think of a way to change the effect of this part?

This is, of course, a fantastic reading comprehension tool. However, for writing, it is a fantastic planning tool. The children can see the language creating effects and then turn that round to use their own language to plan and write high quality texts themselves. The can use a blank chunking grid, focusing on the effect they want to create (it can be the same or different to the model) to write their plan. This works very well, again at many levels. They can stick very closely to the grammar and borrow parts of the text, if they need that level of scaffolding. Conversely, they can be encouraged to simply use a similar variety of grammatical structures, but change the vocabulary and other language features completely. It's up to you to decide!

How to Play Tag

STRUCTURE	CONTENT	LANGUAGE AND PUNCTUATION
Introduction. Four short sentences.	Tells you what the text will be about.	Question (question mark) Exclamation (exclamation mark) Capital letters and end punctuation (full stops, question and exclamation marks) for each sentence.
Numbered instructions	Tells you how to play tag, but breaks it down into careful steps, so it is easy to follow.	Conjunctions to begin most of the sentences: first, now, after that, next Imperative verbs (giving commands) are used to tell you what to do: choose, run, stand, count

A Day in the Life of a Cat

STRUCTURE	CONTENT	LANGUAGE AND PUNCTUATION
Introduction One short paragraph	Tells you what the cat is like Tells you what the cat likes to do Gives an idea of what the rest of the text will be about	Uses specific adjectives to describe the cat: pretty, sweet, lazy Uses effective verbs to show what the cat likes and dislikes doing: play, run/lies around 'I will tell you about...yesterday': adverbial of time so we know when the events happened. Exclamation mark for emphasis
Second paragraph	Tells you what the cat did in the morning: starts at the beginning. Some comments from the writer to show how he/she feels about what the cat is doing Describes how lazy the cat is in the mornings	Uses a conjunction: first Short sentence and exclamation mark: She always is! Adverb: slowly. Effective verbs and verb-noun combinations to show how slow and lazy she is: walked, stretched, took ages
Third, fourth, fifth paragraphs	Tells you what the cat did next, in order of when she did it. Tells the story of the day, from beginning to end. Describes the cat's activities Shows how the writer feels about the cat's activities	Connectives to show how the time moves on: after lunch, then, all that evening Effective verbs and some adjectives: played, watched, twitching, chasing, asleep, lazy Some short sentences with exclamations marks at the end to comment on the cat's activities: 'What a lazy cat!', 'She was too lazy!'

Why Santa Should Upgrade His Sleigh

STRUCTURE	CONTENT	→ EFFECT →	LANGUAGE AND PUNCTUATION
Opening letter conventions	Address and greeting at the top of the page	The address helps the reader know who to write back to.	Everyone knows who it is for. Shows the writer knows how to address a letter correctly and makes the reader want to know what they have to say.	Correct greeting: 'Dear' and using title 'Father Christmas'
First paragraph	'How are you?' etc. Introduction to the topic	Polite, friendly and not too formal. Makes the writer seem nice and makes the reader feel pleased and want to read on. Makes the reader interested in what the writer wants to say.	Shows that the letter is personal and based on one person's opinion. Shows that the letter is speaking directly to the reader. It feels more personal and makes the reader feel more interested.	Uses the pronoun 'I' quite a lot (first person) Uses the pronoun 'you' quite a lot (second person)
Second paragraph	Gives the first point about why the writer thinks Father Christmas shouldn't use a sleigh any more. Explains the point and gives some detail.	Using plenty of detail shows that the writer has thought a lot about the topic and feels passionate about it. The reader feels that the writer knows a lot. This makes the reader more willing to agree with the writer's point of view.	Makes it more personal and direct to Father Christmas Show that the writer cares about the person they're writing to and that the writer is trying to help Father Christmas by writing to him.	Speaks directly to the letter's recipient: 'Santa' Caring adjectives and nouns: 'sensible', 'a struggle'

Why Shops Shouldn't Sell Sweets to Children

STRUCTURE	CONTENT	EFFECT	LANGUAGE AND PUNCTUATION
Opening paragraph	Introduces topic Gives the writer's opinion Linking sentence from first paragraph to second: 'I shall tell you why.'	Helps reader understand what the text is about. Immediately, we know the writer's opinion and we agree or disagree – we engage with the text. Makes you keen to keep reading and see what the writer's reasons are for his/her opinion.	Strong adjectives: terrible, irresponsible Modifying adverbs: simply, very, truly Shows that the writer has a very strong opinion and makes the reader wonder why he/she has such a strong view. Implies that there is no other point of view; tries to present opinion as fact
First argument/point	Gives a point for and then refutes (argues against) it.	Shows what side the writer is on. Tries to prove that people with the opposing view are wrong, because the writer tells us what other people think and then shows that their view is not right by arguing against it.	Contrast between third person at the start and first person in the middle, then inclusive personal pronouns at the end Presents opinions as facts: 'This is clearly not something we can allow.' Exclamation marks. Moves from impersonally stating an idea to personally sharing his/her idea – we instinctively sympathise with 'I' or 'we' over 'they' Makes it seem more reliable and trustworthy Emphasise writer's point
Second argument/point	Same paragraph structure as the previous one – gives a point for and then refutes it.	Repeating this structure makes the writer's point of view stronger. We feel like the arguments for the other side are weak, because the writer briefly mentions them, then spends ages showing why he/she thinks they are wrong.	Long complex sentences giving the other point of view, followed by a short sentence giving the writer's point of view. Pattern of three ('louder and ruder and smellier') Lots of adjectives and adverbs Makes the writer seem to the point when he/she gives his/her own opinion, as if it's totally indisputable. Gives additional detail and seems more trustworthy Very descriptive; shows the emotion of the writer

Teenage Terror Terrifies Toddler

STRUCTURE	CONTENT	EFFECT →	EFFECT	LANGUAGE AND PUNCTUATION →
Headline	Brief overview of story	Creates interest: lack of detail makes reader want to know more and therefore want to read the story.	Makes the sentence more memorable and punchy. The emotive and exaggerated verb makes the reader wonder what on earth the teenager could have done to provoke such a serious reaction in the toddler.	Alliteration: 'T' Hyperbole: strong and effective verb 'terrifies'
Opening sentence	Answers the five **W**s: **who**, **what**, **where**, **why** and **when**.	Provides the details we need to understand the story. Not much more informative than the headline, but a little bit clearer. Reader still interested to know more detail and also shocked at how bad it sounds when it's said so bluntly.	Reiterates the main details of the story: sets up a clear difference between the little toddler and the nasty teenager. Makes the reader immediately sympathise with the child, because the teenager sounds violent and cruel.	Repetition of words used in headline: toddler, terrified/ terrifies, teenage Strong, emotive and affective/effective verbs: 'terrifies', 'broke' (x2) and 'stole'.
Rest of the opening paragraph (lede paragraph)	Gives additional information as to what the current situation is and what other people are doing (i.e. police)	Shows how serious the situation is and makes the reader a bit scared, wondering, if the girl is still out there, where she is. Makes the reader want to read on to find out details of how to stay safe.	Provides a clear description of the girl, making the reader feel like they should be looking out for her. Seems formal; this is official information. Allows the writer to provide a greater level of detail and adds to the formality.	Pattern of three Third person Semi-colons in a list

How do Tooth Fairies Collect Teeth?

STRUCTURE	CONTENT	EFFECT	LANGUAGE AND PUNCTUATION
Introduction – quite short; only three sentences.	Opens by setting up questions in the reader's mind and saying that the answers will be provided in the text: good 'hook' to get reader to read on.	Makes you wonder about the answers to the questions, so creates immediate interest in the text. Connects on a personal level. Strong and specific verb choice.	Personal pronoun 'You' repeated. 'Manages' and 'remove': makes Tooth Fairy's job seems more difficult and, therefore, more interesting.
Rest of text split into sections, each with a sub-heading	Sub-headings break down the process that the Tooth Fairy goes through. All headings are interesting and spark new questions.	Gives a précis version of the process, so the reader can skim quickly and get an idea of what the text will be about. Keeps/creates more interest. Creates/keeps interest and also gives an idea of what each paragraph will be about. Readers can choose to read paragraphs out of order if they so wish. Makes text seem more approachable and easier to read.	Mostly nouns, but specific, well-chosen vocabulary, e.g. 'Magic'
Beginning of first informative paragraph – sub-headed 'The Tooth Gnome"	Immediately starts with what we think we know about the Tooth Fairy and explains why we're wrong	Makes you realize how little you actually know, which makes you feel like you really need to read the rest of the text Makes it clear where you are in the text: helpful 'signposting' Implies that this information is necessary – it's not for fun, it's vital. Seems as if the writer is talking directly to the reader.	"The first thing": adverbial opening. Strong and specific verb choice: 'need'. Personal pronoun: "you"

LANGUAGE AND PUNCTUATION			
CONTENT			
STRUCTURE			

LANGUAGE AND PUNCTUATION			
EFFECT			
CONTENT			
STRUCTURE			

ABOUT TT EDUCATION

TT Education is leading the way in the development and delivery of innovative educational training and products, which make a difference through raising standards in primary schools. Our mission is to motivate and inspire primary teachers, school leaders and children to achieve outstanding results and outstanding schools through engaged learning and visionary leadership.

ABOUT THE AUTHORS

David Maytham

David is a former fast track teacher, education expert and school leader with a proven track record of supporting schools in delivering outstanding results. He was the Lead Writing Teacher at the first Writing Demonstration School in the country and has worked on research projects on behalf of the Department for Education. In 2012, David founded TT Education. He spends his time working with schools across the UK and internationally to raise standards. He runs training days, INSET days and national projects, as well as leading a highly creative team of teachers and other educational professionals to develop exciting and innovative educational resources for schools.

Betsy Maytham

Betsy trained as a secondary English teacher at the universities of Warwick and Reading and worked at schools in Berkshire and Essex before taking up her position at TT Education. She has worked for TT Education since its inception and has created course content and a variety of educational resources, as well as delivering training. Betsy specialises in developing creative and inspiring model texts and teacher support materials.

Index

Index

Index

Index